NATIONAL 4 & 5

MODERN STUDIES

SOCIAL ISSUES IN THE UK

SECOND EDITION

Frank Cooney, Gary Hughes
& David Sheerin

HODDER
GIBSON
AN HACHETTE UK COMPANY

The Publishers would like to thank the following for permission to reproduce copyright material.

Photo credits

p.14 © Ray Tang/Rex Features; **p.15** © 1997 Jules Frazier/Photodisc/Getty Images/ Eat, Drink, Dine 48; **p.16** © Photofusion Picture Library / Alamy stock photo; **p.18** © oneinchpunch / stock.adobe.com; **p.20** © Danny Lawson/PA Archive/PA Images; **p.27** © ALLAN MILLIGAN/AFP/Getty Images; **p.28 (l)** © eye35 / Alamy Stock Photo **(r)** © Kenny Williamson / Alamy Stock Photo; **p.30** © Children's Hearings System; **p.32** © Iain McGuinness / Alamy Stock Photo; **p.33** © gerard ferry / Alamy Stock Photo; **p.35** © EPF / Alamy Stock Photo; **p.37** © Detail Nottingham / Alamy Stock Photo; **p.38** © Martin Brayley / Alamy Stock Photo; **p.42** © Kay Roxby / Alamy Stock Photo; **p.43** © Lebrecht Music & Arts / Alamy Stock Photo; **p.44** © Photographee.eu / stock.adobe.com; **pp.49 and 62** © Gurbuz Binici /Getty Images; **p.56 (l)** © Dave Donaldson / Alamy Stock Photo **(r)** © Roger Gaisford / Alamy Stock Photo; **p.57** © Paul Baldesare / Alamy Stock Photo; **p.60** © Peter Devlin / Alamy Stock Photo; **p.61** © penyushkin / stock.adobe.com; **p.66** © ACE STOCK LIMITED / Alamy stock photo; **p.68** © YAY Media AS / Alamy Stock Photo; **p.69** © Kletr / stock.adobe.com; **p.74** © UK Stock Images Ltd / Alamy Stock Photo; **p.76 (top)** © Ken McKay/ITV/REX/Shutterstock **(l)** © bst2012 / stock.adobe.com **(r)** © Felix Mizioznikov / stock.adobe.com; **p.80** © STEVE LINDRIDGE / Alamy Stock Photo; **p.84 (top)** © JackF / stock.adobe.com **(bottom)** © Kamil Cwiklewski / Fotolia; **p.89 (l)** © sylv1rob1 / stock.adobe.com **(r)** © auremar / stock.adobe.com; **p.92** © Skills Development Scotland; **p.94** © Felix Mizioznikov / stock.adobe.com

Acknowledgements

p.7 Figure 1.1 www.statista.com; **p.7** Table 1.1 https://yougov.co.uk; **p.8** Figure 1.2 https://beta.gov.scot/ **p.9** Figure 1.3 www.ons.gov.uk; **p.13** Paul Lewis, Courtesy of Guardian News & Media Ltd https://www.theguardian.com/uk/2011/sep/05/reading-riots-study-guardian-lse; **p.15** © The Express www.express.co.uk/news/uk/13838/Scots-ministers-Think-when-you-drink; **p.15** www.scotland.police.uk/; **p.20** Crown copyright; **p.21** Crown copyright 2005; **p.22** www.scotland.police.uk/; **p.22** Women's Aid; **p.26** Figure 4.1 www.audit-scotland.gov.uk; **p.27** Adapted from www.scotcourts.gov.uk; **p.30** Figure 4.5 www.scra.gov.uk; **p.32** www.audit-scotland.gov.uk; **p.34** Adapted from www.scotland.police.uk/; **p.37** Courtesy of Robert Gorden University www.rgu.ac.uk/news/school-based-police-officers-reduce-violence-and-support-pupils/; **p.41** Table 6.1 www.prisonstudies.org; **p.45** Adapted from www.scotcourts.gov.uk; **p.47** material adapted by the publisher from *Building a More Equal Scotland: Designing Scotland's Poverty and Inequality Commission* (2017) with the permission of Oxfam, Oxfam House, John Smith Drive, Cowley, Oxford OX4 2JY UK www.oxfam.org.uk. Oxfam does not necessarily endorse any text or activities that accompany the materials, nor has it approved the adapted text; **p.54** Table 8.2 https://researchbriefings. parliament.uk/; **pp.60 and 61** © Trussell Trust; **p.65** Adapted from www. gov.scot/Publications/2012/09/7854/20; **p.66** *Royal College of Paediatricians and Child Health (2017) State of Child Health: Report 2017*. RCPCH: London, 2017. Available at: www.rcpch.ac.uk/sites/default/files/2018-05/state_of_child_health_2017report_updated_29.05.18.pdf; **p.67** Figures 10.3 and 10.4 www.nrscotland.gov.uk; **p.81** © The Herald www.heraldscotland.com/news/15923619. Video_Meals_on_Wheels_services_in_Scotland_at_risk_over_funding_concerns/; **p.91** Figure 11.3 HESA, ECU, IFS; **pp.95–7** © Scottish Qualifications Authority.

Every effort has been made to trace all copyright holders, but if any have been inadvertently overlooked, the Publishers will be pleased to make the necessary arrangements at the first opportunity.

Although every effort has been made to ensure that website addresses are correct at time of going to press, Hodder Gibson cannot be held responsible for the content of any website mentioned in this book. It is sometimes possible to find a relocated web page by typing in the address of the home page for a website in the URL window of your browser.

Hachette UK's policy is to use papers that are natural, renewable and recyclable products and made from wood grown in sustainable forests. The logging and manufacturing processes are expected to conform to the environmental regulations of the country of origin.

Orders: please contact Bookpoint Ltd, 130 Park Drive, Milton Park, Abingdon, Oxon OX14 4SE. Telephone: (44) 01235 827827. Fax: (44) 01235 400401. Email: education@bookpoint.co.uk Lines are open from 9 a.m. to 5 p.m., Monday to Saturday, with a 24-hour message answering service. Visit our website at www.hoddereducation.co.uk. Hodder Gibson can also be contacted directly at hoddergibson@hodder.co.uk

© Frank Cooney, Gary Hughes and David Sheerin 2018

First published in 2013 © Frank Cooney, Paul Creaney and Alison Elliott

This second edition published in 2018 by
Hodder Gibson, an imprint of Hodder Education
An Hachette UK Company
211 St Vincent Street
Glasgow, G2 5QY

Impression number	2
Year	2019

Cover photo © mario beauregard – Fotolia

Illustrations by Emma Golley at Redmoor Design and Integra Software Services Pvt. Ltd

Typeset in 11 on 14pt ITC Stone Serif Medium by Integra Software Services Pvt. Ltd., Pondicherry, India.

Printed in Dubai

A catalogue record for this title is available from the British Library.

ISBN: 978 1 5104 2915 4

Contents

Section 2   # Social inequality

Section 3   # Assessment

Chapter 1

Nature of crime

Unfortunately crime is a part of every society and for those who have been affected by crime, it can be life altering. While some crimes such as theft and assault already feature highly in crime rates, other crimes such as identity theft are on the rise as technology advances.

Nature of crime in Scotland

Due to social issues, such as extreme wealth inequalities, Scotland has an international reputation for violent crime. During the 1980s and 1990s there was a rapid rise in the number of people being assaulted due to a gang culture in Scotland's biggest cities. In 2005, a United Nations report carried out by the World Health Organization highlighted that Scotland had the second highest murder rate in Western Europe and that Scots were three times more likely to be murdered than people in England and Wales. While many would argue that this reputation was undeserved and centred on specific areas, the high levels of crime were without doubt due in part to the use of knives and other dangerous weapons.

Knife crime

At the end of the twentieth century carrying a knife was considered commonplace by people in some of Scotland's poorest areas. The number of people carrying knives appears to have declined across Scotland in the twenty-first century. According to figures from Police Scotland, arrests for the handling of an offensive weapon have been falling sharply, with a decline of 69 per cent over the last decade.

This has had a direct impact on the number of people killed by knife crime. Between 2006 and 2011, 40 children and teenagers were killed in homicides involving a knife in Scotland; between 2011 and 2016, that figure fell to just eight.

What you will learn:
1 The nature and extent of crime in Scotland and the UK.
2 Evidence of crime in Scotland and the UK.

The decline has been greatest in Glasgow, which once had one of the highest murder rates in Western Europe. Between 2006 and 2011, 15 children and teenagers were killed with knives in Scotland's largest city; between 2011 and 2016, none were. This has been due in part to the work of the Violence Reduction Unit (see pages 35–6).

Violent crime

Scotland's reputation as a violent country has also seen a dramatic change in recent years. Violent crimes such as murder and serious assault have fallen, with 2017 seeing reported serious assaults fall below 3000 for the first time in decades. However, violent crime in general continues to rise, with Police Scotland claiming that this is not necessarily due to more violence on Scotland's streets, but due to a change in culture where people are more likely to report violence and an increased chance of successfully convicting violent criminals in court.

Nature of crime in the UK

While Scotland has seen a general fall in serious violent crime this has not been the case across the whole of the UK. In London, in particular, there has been a huge spike in serious violent crime among teenagers. In 2018 the number of teenagers being killed was the highest for more than a decade.

In April 2018, the Commissioner of the Met Police (London Police) publically declared that they 'had not lost control of the streets' following a spate of murders across the city. In the first three months of the year the Met had opened 48 murder investigations, which placed it ahead of New York City for the first time in decades. The vast majority of these crimes were carried out with a bladed weapon, while eight involved the use of a gun.

Evidence of crime in Scotland and the UK

Crime statistics indicate that urban areas with areas of deprivation have the highest rates of crime (see Figure 1.1).

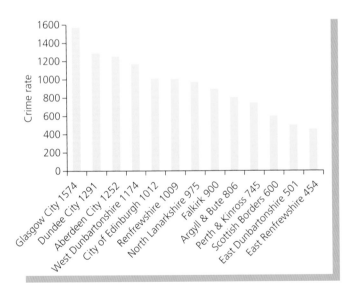

Figure 1.1 Crime rate per 10,000 people by selected local authority, Scotland 2017

Crime by region

Crime and justice is a devolved power for the Scottish Government and therefore it is very difficult to compare crime rates across the whole of the UK.

Show your understanding

1 What evidence suggests that Scotland deserved its reputation as a violent country?
2 Explain, in your own words, why you think Scotland has a problem with knife crime.
3 What evidence suggests that knife crime is declining in Scotland?
4 Why is a rise in the recorded number of violent crimes not necessarily an indication that more crime is taking place?
5 Describe the problems London faced with crime at the beginning of 2018.

Police Scotland analyse their statistics in a different way from other forces in the UK and Scots law means that the way criminals are convicted is also different. However, a YouGov poll (carried out by a surveying company) found that there was a huge variation in how safe people feel in cities across the UK.

Area	Percentage of people who thought it was 'unsafe'
Bradford	42
Birmingham	41
London	39
Glasgow	38
Manchester	34
Liverpool	32
Leeds	30
Sheffield	25
Bristol	19
Edinburgh	14

Table 1.1 Perceived safety of cities in the UK, 2014

Recording crime

One factor that needs to be considered when looking at the nature of crime is how it is recorded. The obvious source for crime rates is the government in conjunction with the courts and the police. However, over time, laws can change and as a result it can be difficult to compare crime rates. The Scottish Government annually releases crime rates and these often appear in the media.

The Scottish Government also releases the Scottish Crime and Justice Survey (SCJS), which includes official measures of criminal convictions and reported crime, and also the public's opinions of crime. This gives a clearer view of crime within the country.

For example, the survey for 2016–17 showed that 86.6 per cent of adults within Scotland did not experience any crime. This highlights that the vast majority of people do not encounter crime and gives a more fair view of crime in Scotland. However, the survey also highlights that only 37 per cent of crime is actually reported to the police, so there is a lot of hidden crime taking place within Scottish society.

Some of the key statistics within the SCJS give an indication of the nature of crime within Scotland.

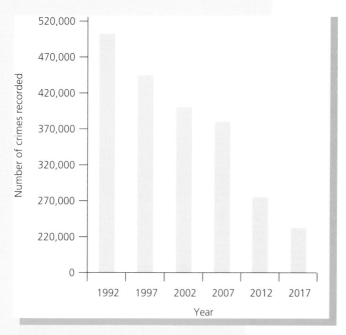

Figure 1.2 Crimes recorded by Police Scotland, 1992–2017

Type of crime	Number of crimes committed in Scotland in 2017
Non-sexual crimes of violence	7,164
Sexual crimes	10,822
Crimes of dishonesty	113,205
Fire-raising, vandalism, etc.	52,514
Other crimes	54,916

Table 1.2 Crime rates by type of crime, 2017

68% of crime is property crime
32% of crime is violent crime
There has been a 38% fall in property crime since 2008
There has been a 27% fall in violent crime since 2008
More than 4 out of 5 violent crimes were committed by males
77% of adults reported feeling safe walking alone after dark
Bank card fraud is the crime most people feel worried about (52%)

Table 1.3 Selected statistics from the SCJS, 2016–17

As England and Wales have a separate legal system they have their own statistics on crime.

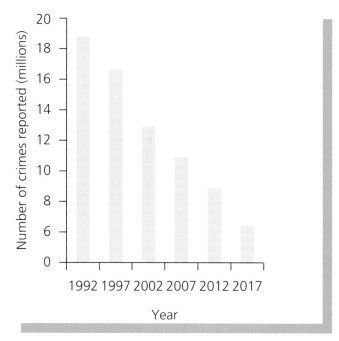

Figure 1.3 Reported crime in England and Wales

Show your understanding

1 Referring to Figure 1.1 on page 7, what explanations can you give for the differences in crime rates across different areas?
2 Why are there difficulties in comparing crime statistics across the UK?
3 Which area feels least safe in the UK?
4 What is the trend in crime rates for Scotland? Justify your answer.
5 Referring to Table 1.2, create a table listing some of the crimes that you think would be included under each of the five crime headings. Aim for at least two different crimes per section.
6 Why is the Scottish Crime and Justice Survey seen as a more accurate picture of crime than crime rates alone?
7 Explain two reasons why some crime is unreported.
8 What is the trend in crime across England and Wales?

Chapter 2

Causes of crime

Studying why people commit crime is called criminology and it was the fastest-growing degree in UK universities in 2018. The decision to commit crime is an individual one and as such people should be responsible for their own actions. However, there are many factors that lead someone to put their freedom at risk and commit a crime. Some people say that the environment an individual comes from – the influences in their life – causes them to commit crime. This provides a **social** explanation of crime. Others will point to financial pressures and greed as factors that influence people to commit crime. This provides an

What you will learn:

1 Explanations of social causes of crime.
2 Explanations of economic causes of crime.
3 Explanations of biological causes of crime.

economic explanation of crime. Lastly, there are some people who point to genetic influences and traits as evidence that, from birth, some people are more likely to commit crime than others. This provides a **biological** explanation of crime.

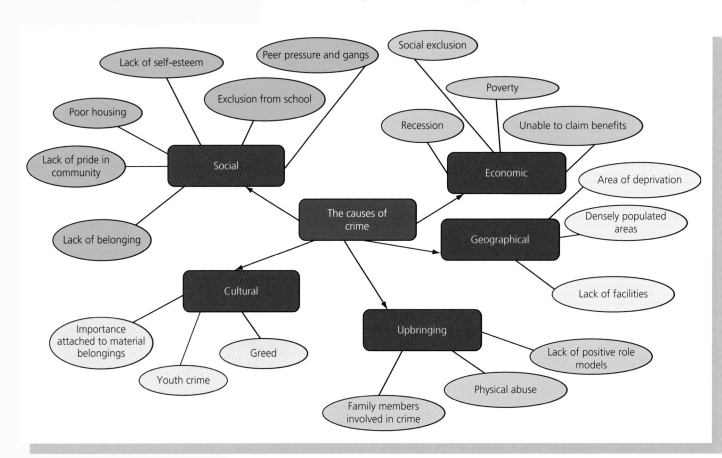

Figure 2.1 Possible causes of crime

Social explanations of crime

When considering the impact of society on developing criminality in individuals, it is important to understand that the various factors rarely act in isolation. A complex combination of factors lead people to commit crimes. For example, the vast majority of people who suffer poverty will never commit a crime.

Family structures

One explanation for criminal behaviour put forward by some criminologists is the changing nature of families in modern-day Britain. The stereotypical family image – mother, father and two children in a detached or semi-detached house – is fast becoming less common. The 2011 census revealed that a greater proportion of the UK's households now comprise single parents, adult children living with their parents, or pensioners than in 2001. There has been a 9.5 per cent increase in single-parent families, up from 2.6 million to almost 2.9 million. Single-parent families make up almost 17 per cent of all families in the census, up from 16.3 per cent in 2001.

There is great debate over the impact of these changes on society and specifically on the increase in youth crime in urban areas within the UK. The Conservative Government shed light on this after their 2010 General Election victory and promised to fix 'Broken Britain'. The secretary of state for work and pensions at that time, Iain Duncan Smith, highlighted on a trip to Easterhouse, Glasgow why some children from complex families may be more likely to turn to deviant behaviour. He stated that due to complex family structures they will develop at a rate that is quite different from those who are growing up in a balanced environment in which there is empathy, reading and conversation; in which somebody has aspirations for the children and a set of values that are passed down to the children.

Youth crime

In the latter half of the twentieth century there was an increase in youth crime in the form of gang violence. Terms like 'ned', 'yob', ASBO and 'hoodies' were used to grab headlines. Many people see external factors such as poverty, poor parenting and peer pressure as reasons for young people committing crime. Young people generally are finding their way in the world and in Scotland are not considered fully responsible for their actions until they are sixteen. Therefore external factors are thought to be more responsible for leading younger people down a path of criminality. There is no simple combination of circumstances that results in criminality in young people, but there are a number of key risk factors that may result in youth offending. These are:

- being male – 87 per cent of youth crime is committed by males
- having parents or other family members who are perpetrators or are imprisoned
- suffering bereavement or family breakdown
- drug and alcohol misuse
- neglect and even physical, sexual or emotional abuse
- associating with other young criminals
- witnessing domestic violence.

Alcohol and drug abuse among parents has been identified as one of the main reasons for these 'troubled youngsters'. The types of crimes committed most regularly are breach of the peace, followed by vandalism and assault. Young people are responsible for higher proportions of offences such as fire-raising (86 per cent), vandalism (75 per cent), theft of motor vehicles (75 per cent), handling offensive weapons (59 per cent) and housebreaking (55 per cent). It is estimated that the bulk (49 per cent) of youth crime is attributable to those aged 18–21. The under-15s commit over one-third of youth crime, with the remainder attributable to those aged 16–17.

Gangs

When considering young criminals we normally associate their actions with gangs. Recent studies have found that up to 3500 young people between the ages of 11 and 23 have joined one of the 170 street gangs within Glasgow's borders. Furthermore, the homicide rate for Glasgow males between the ages of 10 and 29 is comparable to the rates in Argentina, Costa Rica and Lithuania. The reasons why young people join gangs are varied, but invariably they are related to problems in their lives and in the local area.

Education

There is an argument that a lack of education can lead someone down a path towards committing crime. Students from the poorest areas are more likely to have additional support needs; to leave school as a NEET (a young person not in education, employment or training) and their levels of attainment will be lower than those from better off areas. School exclusion rates are higher in local authorities with higher levels of poverty.

Students get excluded from school for a variety of reasons. Many young people in this situation may feel abandoned by their teachers and even their parents and may find comfort in belonging to a gang.

This pattern is also reflected in attainment. In Scotland, attainment is measured by SQA (Scottish Qualifications Authority) examination results. Students from the poorest backgrounds do less well on average than those from areas that suffer less deprivation. The reasons for these statistics are wide-ranging and extremely complex. Students from poorer areas such as Drumchapel in Glasgow and Bowbridge in Dundee may find that education is not a priority. Gang culture, criminality in parents, family violence and abuse and poor upbringing can all contribute to a lack of focus on attainment. For some of these young people who perform poorly in school a life of crime is seen as a preferred route to wealth and material objects than struggling on a low income and perhaps a greater risk of unemployment.

Reasons why some people join gangs

- **A sense of 'family'** – Young people might feel that they don't receive enough support or attention at home.
- **Need for food or money** – Increasingly, gang members use their affiliation to make a profit through illegal activities, such as selling drugs and theft.
- **Desire for protection** – Communities with high gang activity often see young people join a gang just to survive.
- **Peer pressure** – Kids and teens face constant pressure to fit in.
- **Family history or tradition** – Families can have gang involvement spanning multiple generations.
- **Excitement** – Many teenagers from areas of deprivation cannot afford to take part in activities that stimulate them, or such activities may not be available in their areas. This **social exclusion** (see pages 52–3) can lead them to seek thrills elsewhere.
- **To appear cool** – Being part of a gang offers instant respect and a way to access loyal friends.

Show your understanding

1 What are the three main explanations for crime?
2 According to the last census, how have family structures changed?
3 In your own words explain why, in some cases, the changes to family structures may influence some young people towards a life of crime.
4 Look at the key factors that influence youth crime. Chose three and explain why they may negatively influence a young person.
5 What types of crime are young people more likely to commit and why do you think this is the case?

Case study: London riots

Opinion differs on the causes of the 2011 riots, which began in the London boroughs and spread to Manchester, Birmingham, Bristol and Liverpool. A *Guardian* article at the time stated that the riots represented 'the most serious bout of civil unrest in a generation'. Five people died and more than 2500 shops and businesses were damaged. More than 2000 participants in the riots were arrested and 1400 were sent to jail.

On 4 August 2011 Mark Duggan, a 29-year-old black man from Tottenham in London, was shot and killed by police. He was suspected of being in possession of a handgun. Mark's death led to a public protest in Tottenham over the circumstances of his killing. It was a peaceful protest, but later that night violence broke out.

Some argue that this event sparked the riots, but the events that followed were not race riots. 'Reading the Riots', a joint study by the *Guardian* and the London School of Economics (LSE), looked into the causes of the 2011 riots.

Professor Tim Newburn, head of LSE's Social Policy Department, felt that it was very important to speak with those involved in the riots, including the police and victims. In interviews with the rioters, 85 per cent of those questioned said policing was an 'important' or 'very important' factor in why the riots happened.

Here are some of the responses given by those involved in the riots:

- 'The police is the biggest gang out there.'
- 'Abuse of police power in their communities.'
- 'They just generally class you as someone that's bad like that.'
- In response to the question 'Do the police in your area do a good or bad job?' only 7 per cent of 'Reading the Riots' respondents said 'excellent' or 'good', compared to 56 per cent of respondents to the same question in the British Crime Survey.
- Of the respondents, 73 per cent said they had been stopped and searched in the past twelve months; they were more than eight times more likely than the general population in London to have been stopped and searched in the previous year.

In an ICM poll (one carried out by a social research company), while rioters named poverty and policing as the two most important causes of the riots, when the general population was surveyed, poor parenting (86 per cent) and criminality (86 per cent) were said to be the leading riot causes. One newspaper columnist blamed 'feral parents [who were] too drunk or drugged or otherwise out of it' to care if their children were out looting and burning.

Gender and the riots

Government data has estimated that only 10 per cent of those who took part in the riots were female. But the 'Reading the Riots' research indicates that girls and women appear to have played a significant role in the disorder. In the study, interviews carried out with female rioters revealed complex reasons for their involvement. Similar to the men who rioted, some were there only to loot and exploit the anarchic situation; others said that they had no intention of stealing and that they got caught up in the moment.

→

Social networking and the spread of the riots

During and immediately after the riots, many media reports claimed that social media played an important part in inciting, organising and spreading the riots. Some politicians and commentators called for Twitter to be closed down, but studies have shown that there is no significant evidence of Twitter playing such a part. In fact, it was found that Twitter proved valuable in mobilising support among people who volunteered to clean up.

Free mobile phone messaging did provide a fast and free method of communication, however, and seems to have been used by many who took part in the riots.

Poverty and the riots

Home Office research found that those appearing at court in the aftermath of the riots tended to be from more deprived circumstances than the wider population of England:

- 35% of adults were claiming out-of-work benefits (compared to 12% of the working-age population).
- 42% of young people brought before the courts were eligible for free school meals, which are only available in England to the 16% of secondary school students from the poorest backgrounds.
- 58% of those appearing in court identified their residential location as being within the 20% most deprived areas in England.
- 46% were black mixed race and 42% were white.
- 75% had a previous conviction.
- 90% were male.

The police point of view

Officers interviewed as part of the study said further disorder was likely, with many commenting on the cutbacks to public services and welfare benefits as possible causes.

The prime minister's view

David Cameron, the prime minister at the time, said: 'These riots were not about poverty. That insults the millions of people who, whatever the hardship, would never dream of making others suffer like this … [it comes down to] a lack of proper parenting, a lack of proper upbringing, a lack of proper ethics, a lack of proper morals.'

Figure 2.2 A scene from the riots in England in 2011

Alcohol and drugs

Alcohol abuse is linked to many crimes, especially violent crimes. Nearly half of all of Scotland's prisoners say that they were under the influence of alcohol at the time of their offence. While this is a problem across the UK, it has been identified as a particular issue for Scotland. According to former Justice Secretary Kenny MacAskill: 'we in Scotland have a cultural problem with alcohol. Too many Scots think it is acceptable to get drunk. Abused partners, random assaults, stabbings and vandalism – the impact is there for all to see – on the streets, in the police stations, in hospital emergency departments, and in the courts.'

Case study: One Punch Two Lives

Police Scotland runs a number of programmes to raise awareness of the relationship between alcohol and violence. One such programme is called One Punch Two Lives and aims to target those who commit violent crime while on a night out.

When launching the campaign in 2017, Assistant Chief Constable Mark Williams said: 'Drinking too much can make you vulnerable and it increases your risk of becoming a victim of crime or getting into trouble. One punch can kill and could result in you facing a jail sentence. I want people to enjoy their nights out but at the same time to drink responsibly and consider how much alcohol they are consuming and the effect it has on their decision making and judgement.'

Cabinet Secretary for Justice Michael Matheson said: 'Identifying and tackling the root causes of crime and the issues that cause harm in our communities is a responsibility for the police, our partners and communities. The One Punch campaign is part of the Action Against Violence campaign and I am encouraged by this initiative to reduce the number of violent incidents and improve the safety and well-being of individuals and communities.'

Show your understanding

1 Create a detailed mind map explaining some of the key reasons why some young people join a gang. Use illustrations to support your map.
2 What does the term 'NEET' stand for?
3 What is the link between attainment and poverty?
4 Why might some young people who do not do well in school turn to a life of crime?

Academics at Glasgow University have found that people living in an area with six alcohol outlets or more can expect crime rates twice as high as those in an area with only three. The 2015 Scottish Crime and Justice Survey found that 17 per cent of violent crime took place near a pub or club and in 54 per cent of violent crime the perpetrator (offender) was under the influence of alcohol. Karyn McCluskey, co-director of the national Violence Reduction Unit, said: 'Scotland has an incredibly complex relationship with alcohol … People drink for so many reasons but that includes alienation and hopelessness. Too many places are selling alcohol and alcohol is linked to crime.'

In a similar way to alcohol, drugs also have an impact on the causes of crime, especially for young people brought up in an environment of drug abuse. Drug abusers are more likely to commit crimes such as burglary and theft, in order to fund their habit. However, it is highly debatable whether drugs actually lead people to commit crimes or whether those who use drugs are predisposed to such activities anyway.

Figure 2.3 Alcohol abuse is strongly linked to crimes of violence

Added value

'The minimum unit pricing of alcohol will reduce crime.'

Research this government measure and look into the arguments for and criticisms of it. (See also Chapter 10, pages 75–6, for more information.)

Economic explanations of crime

Economic factors/poverty

The impact of poverty on someone's life experiences can be vast. When we describe a group of people from poorer backgrounds we often use the term 'disadvantaged' and this relates to education, housing, social exclusion and even self-esteem. While there is no direct link between poverty and crime there are trends that would suggest some sort of relationship. The Scottish Index of Multiple Deprivation (SIMD) – which looks at a variety of factors that define how much poverty is experienced in different areas in Scotland – shows that Scotland's most deprived areas experience more crime than other areas. Glasgow, West Dunbartonshire and Renfrewshire contain some of the largest areas of social deprivation and suffer from the highest violent crime rates.

Figure 2.4 Crime is more likely to occur in poorer areas

The United Kingdom Peace Index, created by the Institute for Economics and Peace in 2013, ranked Glasgow as the UK's most violent area. The index stated that gangs and knife crime contribute to Glasgow's position and highlighted the link between crime and poverty by describing Glasgow as one of the poorest areas of the UK.

White-collar crime

Some crimes are committed purely out of greed. The perpetrators of these crimes may be comfortably rich but they continue to break the rules in an attempt to increase their wealth. White-collar crime includes fraud, embezzlement or other illegal schemes in the financial sector. Tax evasion is the most popular white-collar crime and there have been a number of high-profile cases in recent years. According to the accountancy firm KPMG the typical fraudster is male, is aged 36–45, holds a senior job in finance, has worked for his company for more than a decade and acts in collusion with a partner.

White-collar crime is non-violent, not obvious and rarely committed against one victim. As a result it is very hard to detect and prove. A few recent examples of individuals who committed white-collar crimes and were prosecuted are Jurgen Whitehouse, an IT services boss at Ofcom, who was sentenced to two and a half years in prison for defrauding the telecoms regulator out of more than £500,000, and a Sainsbury's IT manager who stole millions of Nectar points after finding a loophole in the system and was jailed for twenty months.

 Show your understanding

1 Describe some of the ways in which poverty can impact on people's lives.
2 What evidence is there to suggest that crime is more prevalent in areas of higher poverty?
3 What types of crime do you think are likely in areas of deprivation? Can you explain why?
4 What is white-collar crime? Give an example.
5 Explain why some people commit white-collar crime.

Debate

6 'White-collar crime is not as serious as violent crime.'
Hold a class debate about this statement.

Biological explanations of crime

We have seen how someone's life experiences can lead them down a path of criminality. There is, however, another school of thought that looks at the biological profile of perpetrators and suggests that some of us are born more likely to commit criminal acts, that social experiences and economic conditions only bring out something that already exists within us.

Many people with mental health needs end up in the criminal system. Derek McGill, former governor of HM Prison Barlinnie said he could fill an entire hall at the prison with people who have mental health problems. A 2008 report from Scotland's then chief inspector of prisons, Andrew McLellan, warned that high numbers of people with mental health problems were ending up in prison and that it was not the appropriate place for them.

Mental health

Evidence suggests a link between imprisonment and those with conditions such as ADHD (attention deficit hyperactivity disorder) and depression. A young person struggling to control their ADHD may fail first at home, then at school, then at work and finally with the law. This pattern of troubled lives for children with ADHD is a growing concern, and the proportion of people in jails who have ADHD is estimated to be high. However, mental health and imprisonment is an area of huge debate. A study conducted by Edinburgh University into all of Scotland's prisons found that there is little evidence that significant mental illness is common in the prison population.

Gender

There are key patterns of criminal behaviour in men and women. Men commit far more crime than women. According to the latest statistics, men committed 77 per cent of crimes in Scotland in 2017. Men also dominate violent crimes such as homicide and serious assault. Of women convicted of crime, the largest proportion committed theft. Women are more likely to commit low-level, non-violent offences and therefore pose a lesser risk to society. This may be explained through biological differences between men and women. Women have lower testosterone levels and therefore tend to be less aggressive. However, while crime rates for men have gradually declined, those for women have increased, especially for more serious offences such as assault. This is sometimes linked to the 'ladette' culture.

Figure 2.5 In recent decades there has been a rise in the number of crimes committed by so-called 'ladettes'

'Ladettes' are young women who act in a way that is usually associated with deviance in young men – heavy drinking, drug abuse and assault. UK Government statistics show that youth offending has increased for young women over the past decade, with 22 per cent more crimes committed by girls aged 10–17. While the number of offences involving girls under eighteen has risen by 22 per cent, the number of offences committed by teenage boys has fallen by 9 per cent. Many factors have been blamed for the increase in violent crime committed by women, including a change in the role of women in society.

Case study: Jamie Bulger murder – nurture versus nature

On 12 February 1993 a toddler was abducted from a Merseyside shopping mall by two ten-year-old boys. A shopping-centre surveillance camera had caught two shadowy figures leading away a smaller figure, his hand placed trustingly in theirs. Two days later, James Bulger's mutilated body was found on a railway line. The two-year-old had been attacked with bricks and an iron bar, then laid across the tracks to make it look like an accident.

Jon Venables and Robert Thompson were found guilty of the murder of James. Both were released with new identities when they turned eighteen. While it is thought that Thompson has been rehabilitated successfully, Venables has since been convicted on several charges and has been in and out of prison.

Both boys came from complex family backgrounds, had been failing in school, had a history of violence and had been brought up in areas of multiple deprivation.

 ### Show your understanding

1 Explain why some people would argue that there is a biological link to crime.
2 Explain the links between mental health and crime.
3 What types of crime are men more likely to commit and what types of crime are women more likely to commit?
4 What have been the main changes in female crime in the last few decades?
5 Explain the term 'ladette' in relation to crime.
6 Explain the reasons why the murder of James Bulger can be seen as a 'nurture versus nature' case study.

Chapter 3

Consequences of crime

The consequences of crime can be far-reaching. For most crimes there is a victim or group of victims but the financial and emotional impact of the crime on everyone involved can be difficult to measure (see Case study: Reamonn Gormley). There are also consequences for the person who commits the crime, the perpetrator or offender. In addition, some crimes affect community confidence, which can have a knock-on effect on businesses in the area, particularly if the area is then perceived to have a high crime rate. Crime can therefore have a huge impact on society.

> **What you will learn:**
> 1 The impact of crime on victims, families and perpetrators.
> 2 The impact of crime on communities and on wider society.

Impact of crime on the perpetrator

Many criminals spend time in prison, which should act as a deterrent to committing future crimes as well as a rehabilitative step towards becoming a law-abiding citizen. However, committing a crime can have huge personal consequences for perpetrators as well as impacting on their families.

Once their punishment has been served many convicted criminals find life extremely difficult. They often suffer from a lack of employment opportunities as they must reveal their criminal past when applying for jobs and it is estimated that seven out of ten employers would not employ a convicted criminal. Travel to and from other countries can also be affected. The USA and Australia have particularly robust visa application procedures and if an applicant has a criminal record it is likely that they will be denied access. Mortgage and insurance applications also require people to detail any previous convictions and again this can result in rejection or increased costs. A conviction can also have considerable impact on perpetrators' personal lives, as they may struggle to hold down long-term relationships and to build trust in friendships or within their community.

The families of perpetrators can also be impacted by their crimes. Depending on the specifics of the offence, families can experience shame and embarrassment, be targeted in bullying or revenge attacks and even be forced out of their community. Having a child who is a convicted criminal can impact on the position of parents within their community for the rest of their lives.

Consequences of crime for victims

Crime has obvious consequences for the victims of crime. Depending on the type of crime, this may be physical damage and/or an emotional response. Many people feel a sense of annoyance or anger at **property crime**. In contrast, violent crimes can bring about severe reactions such as anxiety and depression. According to the Scottish Crime and Justice Survey 2016–17 property crime caused the most annoyance (61 per cent), followed by violent crime (51 per cent). Victims also reported experiencing shock (50 per cent) and anger (49 per cent).

Property crime usually involves the damage to or theft of something belonging to someone. This can include burglary, car theft and damaging property. Arson, when someone sets fire to property, is a common property crime.

Case study: Reamonn Gormley

Figure 3.1 The funeral of Reamonn Gormley

In July 2017, Glasgow's *Evening Times* reflected on the 2011 murder of Reamonn Gormley and the impact of his death on family, friends and the local community. The judge in the case described Reamonn as an 'exceptional young man'.

In February 2011, Reamonn Gormley was brutally murdered by two men, one of whom had been released early from a jail sentence. Reamonn had refused to hand over his mobile phone and wallet. Daryn Maxwell was jailed for 19 years while Barry Smith was locked up for just over 8 years. Barry Smith was given the shorter sentence because he did not actually stab the victim.

Reamonn was a student at Glasgow University and during his gap year had taught children in Thailand. His murder had a devastating impact on his family, who made the following statement: 'a loving and kind young man who would have … continued to make a significant contribution to our society, is no longer with us, yet two individuals who have contributed

nothing positive to society but only spread fear and violence will one day be free to walk our streets again.'

Over 2000 people marched through the streets of Blantyre in support of the Gormley family. John Tierney, the local organiser of the march, said: 'One of the most important things is the Gormley family know the community are behind them.'

Show your understanding

1 What difficulties do perpetrators face after they have been convicted of a crime?
2 What is the impact upon the families of some perpetrators?
3 Describe two situations in which a victim may have an emotional response to a crime.
4 Describe the impact of Reamonn Gormley's death on his family and community.

While there are different emotional responses depending on the type of crime, these responses will vary hugely depending on different groups of victims.

Groups most likely to be victims of crime:
- Those in poverty
- Young people
- Elderly people

Those who live in the poorest 15 per cent of areas experience more crime than those in the rest of Scotland. They are more likely to be victims, and are also more likely to be repeat victims. Those in poverty are twice as likely to be victims of crime. Former director of the Institute of Public Policy

Research, Nick Pearce commented that 'people in poorer households have less choice over where to live, they cannot afford to pay for expensive alarm systems or the safety of a taxi ride home. They are less able to control the risks they face and often have no option but to expose themselves to greater danger'.

When it comes to the types of crime, young people are more likely to be victims of violent crime. The most common forms of crime experienced by young people are assault without injury followed by personal theft. This may be due to young people having many desirable and expensive goods in their possession. Mobile phone theft is the most common type of theft in the UK today. Also, young people are more likely to feel pressurised into joining a gang, which brings with it the danger of experiencing crime. In some areas those who refuse to join a gang face greater victimisation, and for those who do join a gang, there is a greater risk of being a victim of a crime as well as committing a crime. Lastly, children are more likely to be victims of mental, physical and sexual abuse. In 2017, ChildLine counsellors dealt with 1.4 million contacts from children about various problems including bullying, sexual abuse, violence and mental health issues.

While older people are statistically less likely to be victims of crime, the impact of crime against elderly people can be devastating. The charity Age Concern found that almost half of those over 75 are too afraid to leave their homes after dark because they believe they would be subject to verbal abuse or muggings. Two thirds feel that they will inevitably become victims of crime as they get older, while one fifth stated that this fear has caused a sense of loneliness and isolation.

In recent years criminal gangs have targeted elderly people by attempting to trap them in a financial scam – using their vulnerability to extract life savings and other assets that they might possess.

SCAM TARGETS THE ELDERLY

In recent years fraudsters have targeted elderly people with various scams that aim to gain access to life savings and other investments. One such scam is 'vishing'. This scam involves the criminal posing as a legitimate organisation linked to the victim – usually a bank or building society – and often preys on the fears that some elderly people have about online banking. The scammers contact the victim via telephone, claiming that the victim's account has been 'hacked' or that their credit card has been 'cloned', and trick the victim into revealing personal information that allows their bank accounts to be accessed. Those who fall victim to the crime can have their life savings wiped out in less than 24 hours. It is estimated that vishing has cost victims £7 million per year. Financial Fraud Action estimates that 43 per cent of victims were over 50 years old.

 Show your understanding

1　What are the key statistics that show that people in poverty are more likely to be victims of crime?
2　Explain some of the reasons why younger people are more likely to experience crime.
3　In what ways do elderly people experience crime?

 Added value

'Crime has the greatest impact on the young'.

Consider the arguments for and against this hypothesis (viewpoint). Do those in poverty or elderly people also face issues?

Consequences of crime for families

While women in the UK commit far less crime than men, they are often the victims when it comes to violent crime. According to the pressure group the Fawcett Society at least one in four women experience domestic violence in their lifetime, and between one in eight and one in ten women experience it annually. These figures relate only to reported crimes – and less than half of all incidents are reported to the police, though this still amounts to one domestic violence call every minute in the UK. Violence against women is still persistently high despite a number of government campaigns.

SCHEME TO HELP PREVENT DOMESTIC ABUSE

In October 2017 Police Scotland launched The Disclosure Scheme for Domestic Abuse Scotland. The scheme aims to empower both men and women with the right to ask about the background of their partner, a potential partner or someone who is in a relationship with someone they know, when there is a concern that the individual may be abusive. In the past, it could have been difficult for someone entering a new relationship to find out whether their partner had prior convictions for violence or domestic abuse.

The scheme aims to enable potential victims to make an informed choice as to whether to continue the relationship, and provides further help and support when the potential victim is making that choice.

'Right to Ask' is the powerful message behind the scheme.

DOMESTIC VIOLENCE – A HIDDEN CRIME

Domestic abuse is still largely a hidden crime: victims often try to keep it from families, friends and the authorities. Victims may also find it difficult to leave the abusive relationship, for some of the following reasons identified by Women's Aid.

- Danger and fear: Leaving can be dangerous – there is a huge rise in the likelihood of violence after separation.
- Isolation: Perpetrators will often try to isolate the victim from family, friends and the outside world making it difficult for them to seek support or recognise abusive behaviour
- Shame, embarrassment or denial: Victims may be ashamed or make excuses to themselves and others to cover up the abuse.
- Trauma and low confidence: The abuse they experience means that victims have very limited freedom to make their own decisions.
- Practical reasons: Often victims are left unable to support themselves or their children.
- The support isn't there: Misunderstandings about domestic abuse often prevent professionals from knowing what to do or where to direct victims.

Women are traditionally at the centre of a family and so tend to experience added pressures when it comes to the impact of criminality on the family and also the impact of criminality within the family. In some instances women are left to pick up the pieces in the wake of criminal behaviour from teenage boys and to raise families due to absent fathers who are in prison.

Crime also has an impact on young people within families. According to the children's charity Barnardo's, children who have a parent who is in prison are twice as likely to experience conduct and mental health problems, and are less likely to do well at school. They are three times more likely to be involved in offending. Sixty-five per cent of boys with a convicted father will go on to offend themselves.

Show your understanding

1 In your own words, explain the issues surrounding domestic violence.
2 What do you think are some of the reasons why domestic violence is massively under-reported?
3 Explain in what ways crime can have an impact on the children of perpetrators.

Consequences of crime for communities

Crime can have a very negative impact on local communities. Once an area experiences high crime levels, the impact may be long lasting and span generations. Once a region with a high level of crime is labelled as a 'bad' area it may be permanently damaged in terms of public perception. This means that 'new' families are less likely to enter the area and help to dilute tensions in the community. An example of this is Easterhouse in Glasgow. In the 1980s and 1990s, Easterhouse developed a very bad reputation for gangs and violent crime. The community was divided, with several gangs protecting their 'patches' and there was also a high drug crime rate. Through investment over the past two decades Easterhouse has seen a significant drop in crime and levels of gang activity. There has also been investment in community facilities such as the building of the Fort shopping village and new homes. However, the area still suffers from a bad reputation. House prices continue to be lower than average and unemployment rates continue to be high.

High crime levels can also contribute to 'environmental poverty', with high levels of vandalism and graffiti, which makes the area less desirable and more dangerous. The fear of crime can also deter people from using public facilities such as parks and public transport. Many people in the most deprived areas of Scotland with the highest crime rates suffer from poor health.

Wider consequences of crime

Economic impact

As well as the emotional and physical impact of crime, there is an obvious financial impact. According to the Scottish Government over £2.5 billion was budgeted for criminal justice in 2017–18. This represents the fourth highest area of spending behind health, education and local government.

Dealing with perpetrators inevitably incurs a cost to the taxpayer but there are also financial costs for the victims. Robbery, burglary and criminal damage all incur costs for the victim, but there is also the emotional value attached to some belongings, which cannot be valued. For some individuals these costs are covered by insurance, but, in the long term, this will increase insurance costs for everyone.

Crime results in costs for businesses, as a result of shoplifting and the expense of crime prevention measures such as CCTV and other security solutions. There are on average 2 million incidents of shoplifting a year in the UK retail sector. However, it is not just the cost in lost goods, or the cost involved in insurance that has an impact. The overall economy suffers as these costs are passed to consumers and restrict the ability of businesses to expand and take on new workers.

Political impact

The issue of crime in society is an emotive one and plays a central part in a government's work. Crime has a personal and, at times, brutal impact on people's lives and the media often demand that politicians deal with those who commit crime in particular ways.

One of Tony Blair's most iconic sound bites was 'tough on crime, tough on the causes of crime' and under his Labour Government (1997–2007) there was a huge increase in the prison population. Since then, there has been a 'rehabilitation revolution' during which the coalition government aimed to reduce the prison population in an attempt to reduce costs while still ensuring a tough approach to crime. Generally, the public demand that criminals are dealt with firmly and that they are appropriately punished. There are, however, certain instances when particular criminal acts or issues become central to public debate and as a result the government is forced to react in order to ensure popularity with the voters.

Case study: Clare's Law

Following the death of his daughter Clare in 2009 at the hands of her ex-boyfriend, Michael Brown campaigned alongside other campaigners against domestic abuse for a change in the law. He travelled down from Aberdeen to hand in a petition at 10 Downing Street. As a result, the Domestic Violence Disclosure Scheme was introduced across England and Wales in 2014, which allows partners to find out if their partner has a history of violence.

Show your understanding

1   Explain two ways in which crime can have a negative impact on communities. Make sure you give an example for each.
2   Why might living in a high crime area impact on your health?
3   In what ways does crime have economic consequences for:
    (a) individuals
    (b) businesses?
4   With a partner, consider in what ways crime has political consequences.

Chapter 4

Criminal justice system

Overview of the judicial system

Scotland has two types of court: civil and criminal. In simple terms, civil courts exist to resolve the differences of two parties who have a dispute, in a fair and unbiased manner. In contrast, the function of a criminal court is to provide a means of prosecuting those who are deemed to have broken the laws of society. In both courts, those accused are allowed to plead their innocence and present legal arguments and evidence central to the case. To ensure a case comes to a fair and just conclusion, it is up to a judge or jury to decide a verdict.

What happens when someone commits a crime?

When the police identify a person or persons they think may be responsible for a crime or offence they can decide to take no further action, issue a warning, issue a fine or send a prosecution report to the Crown Office and Procurator Fiscal Service for a procurator fiscal to review. Upon receiving a prosecution report from the police, the procurator fiscal can decide to take no further action (if there is insufficient evidence or if prosecuting is not in the public interest); issue a fine or begin court proceedings. If it is the latter, the procurator fiscal decides where the trial should take place based on the sentences the court can impose and the nature of the crime.

> **What you will learn:**
>
> 1 What happens when someone commits a crime.
> 2 The criminal court system in Scotland.
> 3 The Children's Hearings System.

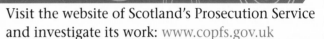

ICT task

Visit the website of Scotland's Prosecution Service and investigate its work: www.copfs.gov.uk

Figure 4.1 provides an overview of an offender's journey through the criminal justice system. This demonstrates the main processes involved and summarises the possible outcomes at different stages. What happens at each stage depends on decisions made by the accused (often on the advice of their solicitor), the various criminal justice bodies and individuals such as sheriffs. In reality, there are many variations in the route through the system and in what can happen at each stage.

> **Show your understanding**
>
> 1 What is the difference between the civil and criminal courts?
> 2 What happens when the police suspect someone of committing a crime?

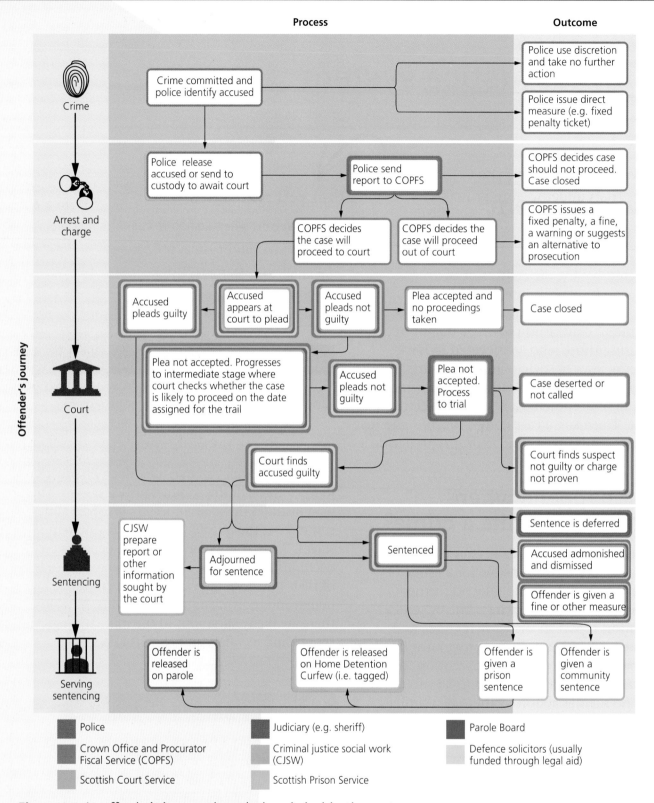

Figure 4.1 An offender's journey through the criminal justice system

Note: Coloured borders round the boxes signify the different bodies generally involved at that stage of the process.

The criminal court system in Scotland

Within the court system there are two types of criminal procedure for hearing cases: solemn and summary.

Solemn cases are concerned with the most serious offences such as murder, rape or serious assault. Trials under solemn procedure are conducted in the High Court or Sheriff Court with a judge and a jury. In Scotland a jury of fifteen decides on the verdict of cases and a simple majority is needed to determine the outcome of the verdict. Citizens of Scotland over the age of eighteen can be called at any time for jury duty.

Summary cases deal with other criminal activity, for example breach of the peace, and are heard in a Sheriff Court or a Justice of the Peace Court without a jury. The vast majority of cases going through the criminal justice system are summary cases – over 90 per cent in 2017.

The procedure in a criminal court

Depending on the court, a judge, sheriff or justice of the peace will normally sit at the head of the courtroom on a raised platform commonly known as the Bench. There may also be a jury if it is a solemn case.

Figure 4.2 Who is present at a court case?

- The prosecutor – in the courtroom the prosecutor presents the evidence in the case against the person charged with the crime.

- The accused – the person who has been charged with the crime is commonly known as the accused.

- The accused's solicitor – accused persons may represent themselves or nominate a solicitor to represent them in court.

- A court official – the clerk of court records the court's proceedings and gives advice on court procedures. However, in the Sheriff Court and High Court, the clerk, who normally sits at the table in front of the judge facing into the courtroom, is not legally qualified and cannot give legal advice.

How does a case unfold in court?

- Making a plea – at the start of a case the accused is asked to plead to the charge or charges they face. If the plea is not guilty, a date will be fixed for a trial when evidence in the case will be heard.

- The trial – at the trial both the prosecutor and the accused can call witnesses to give evidence. After all the evidence has been presented by both the prosecutor and the defence, a decision is taken on the guilt of the accused. In a jury trial, where fifteen people hear the evidence, the jury makes this decision. A majority verdict is required.

- The sentence – if the accused has pled guilty, or has been found guilty after the trial, the court will consider the question of sentence. Various sentences can be imposed by the court (see pages 28–9 for information on sentencing).

There are three types of criminal court in Scotland to deal with different levels of offending.

The three main courts dealing with criminal matters are:

- The High Court of Justiciary
- Sheriff Courts
- Justice of the Peace Courts

The High Court of Justiciary

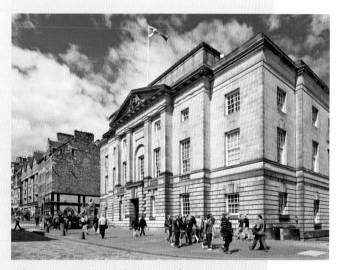

Figure 4.3 The High Court of Justiciary

The High Court of Justiciary is the supreme criminal court in Scotland and deals with the most heinous of crimes such as murder, rape, armed robbery and serious sexual offences, particularly those involving children. It sits in cities and larger towns around Scotland and has a permanent base in Edinburgh, Glasgow and Aberdeen. The High Court is presided over by the lord justice general and the lord justice clerk. When sitting as a court of 'first instance' (this means when hearing a case for the first time rather than on appeal) a single judge, known as a lord commissioner of justiciary, usually presides. In particularly complex or important cases a bench of three judges may preside.

Sentencing in the High Court

The sentencing powers of the High Court are unlimited. Due to the nature of crimes dealt with at the High Court, sentences will always be custodial. For the most serious of crimes, such as murder, statute dictates that life imprisonment be imposed on the accused. However, in Scotland a life sentence is determined by the judge. The average life sentence in Scotland is thirteen years and six months.

Sheriff Courts

Figure 4.4 A Sheriff Court

There are six Sheriffdoms in Scotland with a total of 49 Sheriff Courts spread around the country. A sheriff presides over trials at a Sheriff Court. A sheriff is a solicitor or advocate who has over ten years' experience and considerable courtroom knowledge. The majority of both criminal and civil cases in Scotland are dealt with in the Sheriff Courts. In criminal cases, depending on the gravity of the offence that the accused is charged with, one of two procedures will be adopted – summary procedure or solemn procedure. If the alleged offence is a serious physical assault usually a solemn procedure would be required, which means trial by jury. In civil cases, sheriffs deal with a variety of cases, including cases involving debt, claims for compensation, bankruptcy, company liquidation and eviction. They hear almost all family actions – including divorce, child welfare and adoptions – and have important functions in relation to children's hearings.

Sentencing in Sheriff Courts

In solemn cases, the maximum sentence available to a sheriff is five years' imprisonment and/or an unlimited fine. In summary cases twelve months' imprisonment and/or a fine up to £5000 is available. Note that the case can be remitted to the High Court of Justiciary for sentencing if the sheriff decides that his/her sentencing powers are insufficient.

Justice of the Peace Courts

Justice of the Peace Courts were formerly known as District Courts. Justices of the peace are 'lay magistrates' (not legally qualified) who sit with a legally qualified clerk who advises them in dealing with summary criminal cases. There are around 450 justices, who are drawn from all walks of life. Justices usually sit alone and deal with less serious assault, breach of the peace, theft and other less serious crimes. Further to this they deal with many driving offences such as speeding, careless driving and driving without insurance.

It is worth noting that in Glasgow a slightly different system operates where Justice of the Peace Courts are manned by legally qualified 'stipendiary magistrates'. Like sheriffs, they deal with more serious summary business, such as drink driving and assault. This system is only in place in Glasgow, mainly due to the high volume of crime in the city.

Sentencing in Justice of the Peace Courts

Sentencing powers are limited to 60 days' imprisonment or a fine of up to £2500 or both. Drivers may be disqualified on a discretionary basis. In stipendiary courts magistrates enjoy greater sentencing powers akin to those of a sheriff in summary procedures.

Show your understanding

1 Explain the difference between solemn and summary procedures.
2 What types of crimes are heard at the High Court of Justiciary?
3 Outline the sentencing powers of the High Court.
4 What types of crimes are heard at the Sherriff Court?
5 Outline the sentencing powers of the Sherriff Court.
6 What types of crimes are heard at the Justice of the Peace Court?
7 Outline the sentencing powers of the Justice of the Peace Court.
8 Create a mind map with detailed information on the following:
   • High Court of Justiciary
   • Sheriff Court
   • Justice of the Peace Court

Verdicts in Scottish courts

There are three verdicts that a jury can arrive at in the Scottish criminal courts: **guilty**, **not guilty** and **not proven**. Both not guilty and not proven lead to the acquittal of the accused. The not proven verdict is unique to Scotland and has caused controversy since it was established in 1728. Some the main criticisms of the not proven verdict are as follows:

• The effect of a not proven verdict is the same as that of not guilty. The accused is acquitted but the implication is that they have escaped conviction *only* because of some doubt or lack of evidence. Therefore not proven is incompatible with the presumption of innocence.

• The not proven verdict can be confusing for juries especially as the jury is not allowed to receive guidance on the difference between the two acquittal verdicts.

- It can be argued that not proven is not conclusive and does not give closure to the families of victims or the accused.
- Some see the verdict as a cop-out; a means for juries who are fearful of wrongly sending someone to jail for life to acquit in the face of considerable evidence.

However, there are arguments to keep the not proven verdict:

- The current system works. There is no need to change it – it has been in place for nearly 300 years.
- It leads the jury to focus fully on the evidence presented and to analyse whether this evidence is sufficient to lead to a criminal conviction.
- The verdict gives the jury another option and therefore gives some degree of flexibility.
- If the not proven verdict is taken away there is a possibility of an increase in miscarriages of justice.

 Show your understanding

1. Create a table outlining the arguments for and against the not proven verdict.
2. What is your view on the not proven verdict? Justify your opinion.

Added value

Research the debate surrounding the not proven verdict.

The Children's Hearings System

The Children's Hearings System is the care and justice system for Scotland's children and young people. It is important that children who commit offences, and children who need care and protection, are dealt with in the same system – as these are often the same children.

The Children's Panel — life changing.

Why would a child be required to attend a children's hearing?

A child may have to attend a hearing for a number of reasons – they may be referred by the police, social workers or through education. Committing a crime is only one reason of many; it could be that the child:

- is likely to suffer serious harm to health or development through lack of parental care
- has committed an offence
- is misusing drugs or alcohol
- has behaved in a way that has had, or is likely to have, a serious adverse effect on the health, safety or development of themselves or another person
- is beyond the control of parents or carers
- is not attending school regularly without a reasonable excuse
- has been, is being or is likely to be forced into a marriage or civil partnership.

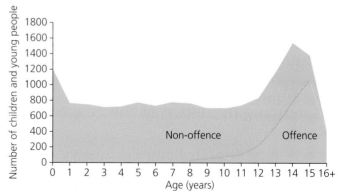

Figure 4.5 Age of children and young people referred to a children's hearing on offence and non-offence grounds in 2016–17

What happens at a children's hearing?

A children's hearing (sometimes called a children's panel) is a legal meeting arranged to consider and make decisions about children and young people who are having problems in their lives. The hearing consists of three members of the local community who act as lay tribunal members, called panel members. They volunteer to sit on hearings. The child and their parent(s) will also be present, as well as a lawyer in some cases. The hearing, which is set up to create a comfortable setting for the child, listens to the child's circumstances and then decides what course of action is required regarding the needs of the child.

The outcome of a panel meeting will vary from case to case depending on the child's circumstances and/or offence. For example, it can require the child to:

- be supervised by the local authority under a 'supervision order'
- stay away from certain locations or individuals
- attend and co-operate with specialist programmes to address their offending behaviour
- live away from home, sometimes in secure accommodation – this is always as a last resort and usually in extreme circumstances.

Only in cases where a young person has committed a serious criminal offence, such as murder or serious assault, will they be dealt with through the court system. The Scottish Government raised the minimum age of prosecution from eight to twelve in the Criminal Justice and Licensing Act 2010. However, the age of criminal responsibility is still eight.

 Show your understanding

1. Give three reasons why a child would be required to attend a children's hearing.
2. Who is present at a children's hearing meeting?
3. Describe the various outcomes that may result from a children's hearing.

Chapter 5

Responses to crime: the police

The structure of the police

Police Scotland is the second largest force in the UK after the Met Police. There are thirteen local policing divisions, each headed by a local police commander who ensures that local policing in each area is responsive, accountable and tailored to meet local needs. Each division encompasses response officers, community officers, local crime investigation, road policing, public protection and local intelligence. The thirteen local policing divisions are:

- Argyll and West Dunbartonshire
- Ayrshire
- Dumfries and Galloway
- Edinburgh
- Fife
- Forth Valley
- Greater Glasgow
- Highland and Islands
- Lanarkshire
- North East
- Renfrewshire and Inverclyde
- Tayside
- The Lothians and Scottish Borders

Alongside the local policing divisions there are a number of national specialist divisions. The Specialist Crime Division (SCD) provides specialist investigative and intelligence functions such as major crime investigation, public protection, organised crime and counter terrorism. These functions may not be required frequently but when a serious crime takes place, or public safety is under threat from criminals, the most professional response is available, regardless of the area in which the crime has taken place. The Operational Support divisions provide specialist support functions such as road policing, air support, dog branch, marine policing and the mounted branch.

What you will learn:

1 The role, structure and powers of the police in Scotland.
2 The effectiveness of the police in Scotland in tackling crime.

FACT FILE

Police Scotland

- Police Scotland is led by a chief constable.
- The chief constable is supported by a command team of deputy chief constables, assistant chief constables and directors.
- The Police Scotland budget in 2017–18 was £1.1 billion – although budget cuts are required over the next few years.
- There are 17,256 police officers in Scotland.
- 6701 police support staff keep the force operational.

The structure of the ranking system within the police works to ensure a chain of command. All police officers begin as constables and have a variety of opportunities to advance up the career ladder. The head of Police Scotland is referred to as the chief constable. The chief constable has overall responsibility for policing in Scotland and is answerable to the Scottish Police Authority. His/her main duties involve:

- direction and control of police officers and civilian police staff
- day-to-day administration and planning within the Police Service of Scotland
- ensuring that all local authority areas have adequate arrangements for policing
- securing best value in the use of resources
- preparation of annual police plans
- a part in the preparation of the strategic police plan.

He/she commands a salary of approximately £215,000 in this role.

The role and powers of the police

Most people would associate the police with responding to emergency situations and keeping the public safe from dangerous criminals. This is true and vital but their role can be extended to preventing crime in the first place, detecting criminals after crime has taken place, educating the public about crime and generally working to maintain law and order at all times. Police Scotland has a specific overall focus to improve the safety and well-being of people, places and communities in Scotland.

Before any prospective police officer is appointed to the role they must make the following declaration:

'I, do solemnly, sincerely and truly declare and affirm that I will faithfully discharge the duties of the office of constable with fairness, integrity, diligence and impartiality, and that I will uphold fundamental human rights and accord equal respect to all people, according to law.'

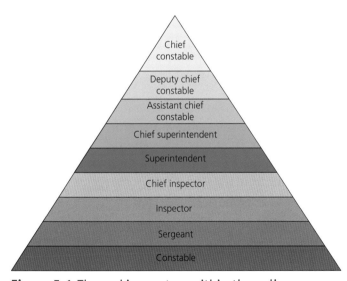

Figure 5.1 The ranking system within the police

Figure 5.2 Police constables on the beat

Show your understanding

1 Describe the structure of Police Scotland.
2 What are Operational Support divisions?
3 Describe the role of the chief constable.

The role of a police constable

Police constables ultimately maintain law and order. They protect members of the public and their property, and prevent, detect and investigate crime. However, being a police officer is a much more complex job than this list suggests. Police constables work to a shift pattern and while this is normally over a 40-hour week it will most certainly involve night working and unsociable hours. Crime is a 24-hour-a-day issue.

Police constables are an integral part of the community – from pounding the beat to providing security at major sporting events, the police need to be ready for any eventuality. A police constable's work is based in and around the local communities that they serve, so it is important that officers are respectful of the culture and beliefs of others. Constables may work in busy city centres and towns or in rural and island communities, both of which have varied and difficult challenges.

Being a police constable can be a challenging and unpredictable job – there's no knowing what you might encounter each day – but it's also a rewarding job. Officers actively make life safer and more secure for everyone.

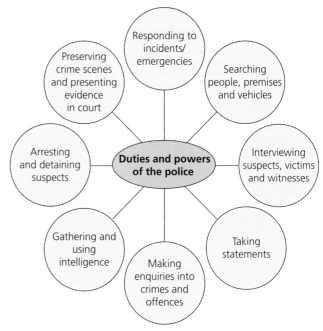

Figure 5.3 Duties and powers of the police

- you are accused by an apparently credible witness of having been seen committing a crime
- you are seen running away from the scene of a crime.

You can also be arrested under specific laws not connected with an offence, for example if you breach a court order to stay away from your former partner.

You can be held in custody for a maximum of 24 hours before the police must either charge you or release you. If, at any time, the police no longer suspect you have committed a crime, they should release you. If it is a very serious charge, you may be held in custody until the next day that a court sits (i.e. Monday to Friday). This means if you are arrested on a Friday you may be kept in custody until Monday morning.

Duties and powers of the police

The police come face to face with the community every day and have a variety of powers to deal with the multitude of situations they encounter.

Power of arrest and detainment

A police officer has the power to arrest you without a warrant (a legal document) if they have reasonable grounds for suspecting that you have committed or are committing an offence. For example if:

- the police officer sees you in the act of committing a crime

Power of stop-and-search

Stop-and-search powers enable the police to dispel or confirm suspicions about individuals and detect, for example, those suspected of carrying weapons, stolen goods or illegal drugs. In practice, the law requires the execution of such powers to be based on fact, information and/or intelligence and not on the whim of individual officers. The age, race or sex of a person, or the officer knowing that a person has previous convictions are *not* good enough reasons to conduct a search. The police have the power to arrest people who are found to be in possession of knives and other types of weapons in public places when they don't have either a reasonable excuse or lawful authority. Police officers will almost always enforce this legislation as knife crimes can have horrific and tragic consequences. Unfortunately young people are frequently involved both as the victims and sometimes the perpetrators of these crimes, therefore young people will be stopped and searched more than other sections of society. The police also have the power to stop and search anyone they believe is a terrorist, or to prevent an act of terrorism. Stop-and-search is generally supported by the public but people often feel victimised if they are stopped and searched themselves.

Figure 5.4 Stop-and-search

Methods of policing and approaches to tackling crime

Police Scotland utilise a variety of different methods and tactics to ensure that society is as safe as possible. The different regions of Scotland have very different needs and challenges. For example, knife crime and drugs are more of an issue in the Greater Glasgow region than in Dumfries and Galloway. Different areas present challenges that require a certain style of policing that best suits the needs of the community. The police also work hard on crime prevention to tackle the root causes of crime.

Crime prevention

One of the most important functions of the police is preventing crime before it happens. Effective policing isn't just about enforcement; tackling the causes of crime is more cost-effective and leads to greater social benefits over a longer period of time. The police work hard to divert potential perpetrators from committing crime in the first place. Much of this work involves the police and associated agencies working with young people and perpetrators to influence thinking and attitudes. The aim is to prevent potential perpetrators turning to crime in the first place or to avoid reoffending.

Show your understanding

1. Describe the role of the police in Scotland.
2. Explain why a police constable might find their role challenging.
3. Copy the police duties and powers mind map (Figure 5.3) into your exercise book.
4. Do you believe that the police should be able to keep suspected criminals in custody for 24 hours? Justify your answer.
5. Describe the power of stop-and-search.

Crime prevention – Violence Reduction Unit

The Violence Reduction Unit (VRU) is a nationwide body that works specifically to reduce incidences of violent crime in Scotland. The VRU works with a whole host of partners, from the police and justice services to education, health and community groups to try and find the best way to make Scotland a safer place to be. In 2010 the VRU had great success with a community initiative to reduce violence in Glasgow's East End, cutting gang crime by over fifty per cent and engaging many youths who felt isolated from society and caught up in gang culture. Today, the number of gangs in Glasgow continues to fall and Glasgow is no longer regarded as the 'murder capital of Europe' although we still have issues to tackle – see information on knife crime, below.

Crime prevention – knife crime

Knife crime in Scotland is a major problem. In Glasgow in particular there is a 'blade culture' where many young people are routinely carrying knives. This had led to newspaper headlines over the last decade describing Glasgow as 'the knife capital of Europe' and 'the most violent city in Britain'. However, over more recent years statistics show that rates of knife crime in Scotland are decreasing. Crimes of handling an offensive weapon (including knives) have dropped dramatically in Scotland, falling by 67 per cent in Glasgow and 60 per cent in Scotland since 2006–07.

In order to achieve such a remarkable drop in knife crime rates both the police and the Scottish Government have intensified crime prevention efforts. The No Knives, Better Lives initiative is a collaboration between the Scottish Government and Police Scotland that works to educate young people about the dangers of carrying a knife and the devastating personal consequences it can have on their future. A range of innovative tactics such as hard-hitting talks in schools, targeted advertising in areas where young people are known to congregate, and youth work interventions, have worked together with tough enforcement on the streets to tackle the issue of knife carrying and knife crime.

ICT task

Visit www.noknivesbetterlives.com and research further how this initiative is helping to reduce knife crime.

Community policing

The public experience of community policing tends to involve police 'on the beat', police attending community meetings and officers assigned to a specific area or town who have the responsibility for building relations in that area. Community policing also takes a problem-solving approach to local issues, often in partnership with other public services, which attempts to get to the root of local problems rather than simply responding to crime by arresting individual perpetrators. Although community policing is part of the service offered by Police Scotland, which recognises its significant successes and public popularity, the police are still predominantly response oriented – answering 101 or 999 calls.

The benefits of community policing include reductions in crime, disorder and anti-social behaviour; increasing feelings of safety among members of the public and improvements in police–community relations. As a community police team becomes familiar with the local residents of a neighbourhood and build relationships with those who live there, evidence suggests that crime rates fall considerably.

However, community policing isn't always successful and can be hard to manage and maintain. It requires interaction with and the involvement of the public, who may have a negative opinion of the police. Community police who are investigating a crime may come up against silence from members of the public even when they have worked hard to build up links and relationships with the local population. Community policing is therefore a long-term strategy that requires a degree of commitment from those involved and a consistent approach to staffing.

Campus cops

As an extension to community policing, police officers have been working with secondary schools across Scotland as 'campus cops'. This involves developing strong links with young people and their communities and changing young people's perceptions of the police. Officers are assigned to schools where they build up relationships with students and staff, providing advice on topics ranging from bullying to drugs. The officers, known as school link officers and school liaison officers in some parts of Scotland, also improve police intelligence on areas surrounding the schools, for example, identifying individuals who have been selling drugs or who are involved in gang-related violence.

Show your understanding

1. Why is it important for the police to focus on crime prevention?
2. Describe the work of the Violence Reduction Unit.
3. Describe the work of No Knives, Better Lives.
4. Explain community policing.
5. Give an advantage and a disadvantage of community policing.
6. Describe the work of a 'campus cop'.
7. Explain the term 'zero tolerance'.

Intensive enforcement

Intensive enforcement or zero-tolerance policing is a tough approach that involves the police clamping down on minor offences in order to reduce low-level offending and make serious crime less likely. In the UK, zero tolerance is based on single issues (such as targeting knife crime in the West of Scotland) and the idea that responding forcibly to crime such as street drinking and knife crime will avert a downward spiral of disorder. However, zero-tolerance policing on a grand scale is at odds with the traditional approach in the UK, where policing is based on a 'service and consent' model rather than the 'crime control' model familiar in the United States. Community policing is another example of the approach in the UK.

Armed policing and Tasers

Figure 5.5 An armed response vehicle attending a crime scene

British police services have never been like their American colleagues, patrolling the beat with a pistol on their hip, trained and ready to shoot if required. The average British police officer goes about his or her duty unarmed, carrying a baton and handcuffs, although sometimes an officer may carry CS spray (a tear gas) and/or a Taser. However, it has been suggested that the traditional unarmed police officer is vulnerable to the threats from gang violence, knife crime, drugs and terrorism posed by modern society and is therefore less effective at protecting the public. All major police forces in Europe (aside from Ireland) and those in the US, Canada and Australia routinely carry firearms, which leaves many questioning whether it is time for UK forces to follow suit. Nevertheless, the various police services around Britain believe they have the correct balance of an unarmed force supported by specialist firearm officers ready to respond when necessary.

An alternative to armed policing is the routine use of Tasers.

The debate over the use of Tasers

Some points to consider in favour of arming all police officers with Tasers:

- Police officers who are issued with Tasers go on a three-day training course and must justify their use.
- Tasers are an appropriate response to a criminal who is brandishing a weapon.
- In some situations where violence is threatened, police officers require a Taser to protect themselves and the public.
- If Tasers were carried by all police officers this would serve as a deterrent to potentially violent criminals.
- Tasers are generally safe and very rarely cause lasting health issues or fatalities.

Some points to consider in the argument against arming all police officers with Tasers:

- If the police were routinely armed with Tasers the police–public relationship would be damaged and the country would become harder to police as a result.
- Critics argue that Tasers can be dangerous and would change the nature of British policing.
- Not all officers are trained in the use of Taser guns.
- There have been cases of fatalities due to the use of Tasers by the police.
- Amnesty International believes that 'Tasers are potentially lethal weapons, which should only be used in serious, life-threatening circumstances and by the highest trained officers.'

Policing methods – Tasers

Figure 5.6 Police with a Taser

A Taser gun uses compressed air to fire two darts that trail electric cables back to the handset. When the darts strike a five-second 50,000-volt charge is released down the cable, causing the suspect's muscles to contract uncontrollably.

A police officer's job is often dangerous and fraught with risk and can involve contact with criminals who may be armed and volatile. Using a Taser, a police officer can disarm a criminal from a safe distance and render the criminal immobile for a period of time to allow arrest. Taser guns inflict a certain amount of pain and discomfort but they are unlikely to kill or seriously harm the individual. However, Tasers have killed people in the past. Any use of a Taser in Scotland is followed up by the police investigations and review commissioner, who assesses whether its use was justified.

national force's first chief constable, stepped down in 2015 after controversies over the high rate of stop-and-searches, the deployment of armed officers to routine incidents, allegations that the force spied on journalists and a bungled response to a motorway accident in which two people died. More recently, the force's second chief constable, Phil Gormley, stepped down from the position amid allegations of bullying and misconduct. Turmoil at the top, along with budget cuts, has meant that Police Scotland has struggled with its public image and suffered poor press coverage.

 Added value

'The police should be armed in the UK.'

Research this hypothesis and come to your own conclusion.

 Show your understanding

1 Outline the arguments for arming the police.
2 Look at the information on Tasers on pages 37–8.
   (a) Describe what a Taser is.
   (b) Create a detailed mind map on the use of Tasers in the UK.
   (c) 'Tasers should be banned, they are too dangerous.'
   Do you agree or disagree with this statement? Justify your opinion.

Issues within the police

As the police are funded mainly by the government and are expected to uphold the laws of society, they are subjected to a level of scrutiny and accountability that no other profession experiences. In a democratic society, elected officials serve to keep the police accountable and to ensure that they reflect the will of the people. As the police enforce the law, it is imperative that they reflect a model of professionalism, fairness, consistency and equality both internally and when dealing with the public. Some specific examples of challenges within the police are as follows.

Police Scotland leadership

Police Scotland has had a rocky start since its creation in 2013, with problems at the very top of the organisation. Sir Stephen House, the

Equality within the police

The police should aim to mirror society in that there should be a gender and ethnic minority balance in staffing. Women are an integral part of a police force, not simply because they make it more representative, but because their presence alone punctuates the macho culture that is sometime associated with police work. At the very least, a police service should be able to relate to the communities it polices; it should be fair and inclusive. In Scotland, women account for 28 per cent of officers and around 20 per cent of all promoted posts. These statistics may seem poor but they are a huge improvement on a decade or two ago when in Scotland the number of women in promoted posts stood at only 8 per cent (less than one in ten).

 Show your understanding

1 What problems has Police Scotland suffered with its leadership?
2 'Police Scotland has a fair gender balance in staffing.'
   Give evidence to support or oppose this view.

Chapter 6

Responses to crime: prisons

The purpose of prisons

In the UK citizens expect to be protected from those who break laws. We expect that those who commit crimes will be punished and that their victims will feel that justice has been done. In the past the punishment for the crime of murder was death. In the UK, however, unlike the USA, the death penalty (capital punishment) is no longer used. At present there is a debate about the effectiveness of a prison sentence and the Scottish Government is introducing radical change to the treatment of women prisoners (see page 43).

What should a prison sentence achieve?

Prison should meet all or some of the purposes outlined in Figure 6.1.

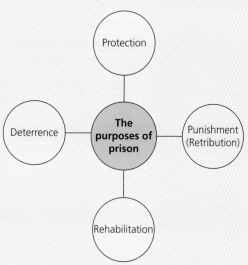

Figure 6.1 The purposes of prison

- Does prison protect the public? It can be argued that if over 90,000 UK criminals are locked up at any one time, they cannot commit a crime.

> **What you will learn:**
> 1 The purpose and effectiveness of prisons.
> 2 The purpose and effectiveness of alternatives to prison.

In reality, this is only short-term security as many prisoners reoffend when they are released. However, for serious crimes such as murder or attempted murder then prison is the only option.

- Does prison provide appropriate punishment and justice for the victim? This is clearly achieved in a custodial (prison) sentence – a prisoner is denied their freedom and separated from family and friends.

- Does prison provide rehabilitation and the support to prevent reoffending? There should be opportunities for prisoners to consider why they committed a crime and a programme of support. Unfortunately, the increase in the prison population and the reduction in prison staff have meant that many prisoners, especially those in jail for six months or less, receive no or very little support. This is referred to as the revolving door of crime.

- Does prison deter the individual from committing a crime? Unfortunately this is not the case as over 70 per cent of short-term prisoners are likely to reoffend. Again, many prisoners suffer mental health and addiction issues (see Profile of Scottish prisoners, page 41), which can contribute to reoffending.

Profile of Scottish prisoners

- Scottish prisoners have low levels of literacy and lower intelligence than the general public.
- Unemployment is thirteen times higher for prisoners on admission compared with the general population.
- Around 70 per cent have histories of poor mental health and/or drug problems.
- Over 25 per cent had been taken into care as a child compared to 2 per cent of the general population.
- One quarter of young male perpetrators in prison are young fathers.
- Half the prison population come from home addresses in 155 of the 1222 local government wards in Scotland.

Country	per 100,000	% Female
Scotland	136	5.0
England and Wales	142	4.7
Norway	74	6.1
Russian Federation	409	7.9
Finland	57	7.7
Poland	197	3.9
France	102	3.5

Table 6.1 Prison population in selected European countries per 100,000 of population and percentage of female prisoners

ICT task

Working in pairs, research the website www.prisonstudies.org. Choose five countries from different parts of the world, for example from Asia and Africa, and compare their prison population to Scotland's. Create a PowerPoint presentation, with between three and five slides, to present to the class.

Scottish prisons

In Scotland there are thirteen publicly managed prisons and two private prisons (Kilmarnock and Addiewell). HMP Polmont provides custodial places for male prisoners between the ages of 16 and 21. HMP Cornton Vale, the main prison for women, is being closed (see page 43).

The Scottish prison population varies from day to day but the average daily number in 2018 was 7440. This is a decline from the high of 7810 in 2010. Only 5 per cent of the prison population is female and for every 100,000 Scots, 136 are in prison. This is a lower figure than in England but much higher than in countries such as Norway (see Table 6.1).

Are prisons failing?

The key question is not *if* but *why* prisons are failing. A range of government decisions have led to changes ranging from longer prison sentences to a reduction in prison staff (cuts to public expenditure). This has caused massive overcrowding, which makes it difficult to provide appropriate rehabilitation programmes and has led to many prisoners being kept in their cells for long periods of time. Add to this the availability of legal and illegal drugs. Many experts claim that the UK prison system is in crisis.

In February 2018 the *Observer* newspaper published the findings of an analysis of 118 prisons in England and Wales. Some of the main findings are shown on the next page.

These findings refer to a study of prisons in England and Wales. The cuts in Scottish prisons have been less severe. Scotland is regarded as being more progressive than England in terms of moving away from custodial sentences for short-term prisoners towards alternatives. By reducing the prison population, the remaining perpetrators could be offered more meaningful rehabilitation programmes (see Case study: HMP Polmont for young offenders). This new approach explains the radical changes taking place in the treatment of women perpetrators (see page 43).

SHOCK FIGURES REVEAL THE DIRE STATE OF BRITAIN'S FAILING PRISONS

- 68 per cent of prisons are now providing unsatisfactory standards of care.
- Every month there are over 40 violent incidents in prisons and every two days a prison officer is assaulted.
- Assaults and serious assaults are at record levels – in the twelve months to September 2017 over 28,000 incidents were recorded, including 7828 assaults on prison staff.
- Rory Stewart, the UK prison minister, stated that prisons are rife with psychoactive drugs that contribute to 'increasing levels of violence committed by prisoners, and horrifying rates of self-harm'.

- On an average day there will be 117 incidents of self-harm and every five days someone commits suicide.
- The number of prisoners in England and Wales rose to 84,225 in February 2018 – in 1993, it stood at 44,552.
- Cuts to the prison service budget by the Conservative Government between 2011 and 2015 have played their part in creating the present crisis. Between 2012 and 2016 as the prison population rose, front-line staff fell by over 7000 (a 30 per cent reduction). Lack of staff leads to many prisoners being locked up in their cells for as long as 23 hours a day.

Case study: HMP Polmont for young offenders

A 2017 report by the chief inspector of prisons praised the wide range of courses that is offered to young offenders, with many leading to qualifications. These included vocational courses on plumbing, joinery, brickwork and painting and decorating. Certification is also provided in catering. Other imaginative courses were on offer, for example young fathers have been encouraged to write and illustrate storybooks for their children.

However, there were some concerns. Despite investment of £3 million in educational facilities only 40 per cent of inmates participated. Many young prisoners spent most of their time locked up because of their challenging behaviour and the existence of rival gang cultures. This is partly because of the dramatic decrease in young offenders being sent to HMP Polmont. (The number of inmates has declined from over 1000 to about 400.) This has increased the percentage of inmates with serious emotional and behavioural issues.

Figure 6.2 HMP Polmont

Radical reform of women's prisons

The Scottish Government has implemented many of the recommendations of the 2012 Angiolini Report, led by Dame Elish Angiolini. This report highlighted that Cornton Vale was not fit for purpose and that prison was not the solution for the majority of the women perpetrators.

In 2017 work began to demolish the 217-cell Cornton Vale prison. It will be replaced by two 'community prisons'.

- On the present site a smaller national facility will be built for about 80 women guilty of the most serious crimes. In 2018 there were about 370 women in custody, down from 450 in 2012. The target is to reduce this to about 230.

- Five new community custodial units are to be built across Scotland. This will ensure that guilty female prisoners will serve their time relatively close to their families. These smaller units will each hold up to twenty women, with the emphasis on rehabilitation. Each unit will have in-house support for mental health and health issues. The women will do their own cooking and laundry and will be able to use local amenities such as swimming pools and gyms and access local health services. Each unit will have a mother-and-child area and children will be able to come and visit and stay overnight.

The emphasis where possible will not be on punishment and deterrence but on recovery and reintegration into society. It is hoped that this will break the cycle of reoffending. Prisons will be a last resort for many women perpetrators, and alternatives to prison such as electronic tagging will be expanded. This is partly in response to the fact that almost 80 per cent of women are sentenced to three years or less for offences that are non-violent.

Women have a better record than men for completing sentences that are alternatives to prison: 95 per cent, compared to only 76 per cent of men.

Figure 6.3 Former lord advocate, Dame Elish Angiolini: 'We sweep these women away and get a temporary reprieve. It's easy but very expensive and very ineffective.'

Prisons are failing women

- Until recently the justice system failed to recognise the difference between male and female prisoners. A 'gender blind' approach discriminates against women. (Men make up about 94 per cent of the prison population.)

- Since 2006, the number of women convicted of a crime in Scotland has risen by 14 per cent but the number in prison have almost doubled.

- Only 2 per cent of women perpetrators have committed violent crime.

- Women are more likely than men to have:
  - mental health and drug problems
  - histories of physical and sexual abuse and victimisation
  - dependent children.

Most women inmates are being locked up for six months or less: over 70 per cent of women sentenced to custody in 2016–17 were given six months or less.

Figure 6.4 Community custodial units will have a mother-and-child area

 Show your understanding

1 Outline the four purposes of prison.
2 Working in pairs, decide if each purpose has been achieved. Give reasons for your decision.
3 Describe the Scottish prison service in terms of prisons, and prisoners.
4 What problems do prisons face in achieving rehabilitation?
5 Draw up a profile of a Scottish prisoner and say to what extent poverty is to blame for their imprisonment.
6 Refer to the extract from the *Observer* on the crisis in prisons in England and Wales (see page 42) and describe, in detail, the problems prisons face.
7 What measures have been introduced at HMP Polmont to assist rehabilitation and what problems does the prison face?
8 Why should women prisoners be treated differently from male prisoners?
9 Describe, in detail, the radical changes in the treatment of women prisoners.

Develop your skills

10 Study Table 6.1 on page 41 and compare Scotland's prison population with that of other European nations.

Alternatives to prisons

In 2014, Lord Carloway, one of Scotland's senior judges, stated that the emphasis in prisons should be on rehabilitation not retribution. In short, alternatives to prisons should be expanded. These alternatives range from fines to Community Payback Orders and Home Detention Curfews (electronic tagging).

Community Payback Orders

The Community Payback Order (CPO) was introduced in 2011 and enables a perpetrator to complete between 80 and 300 hours of supervised work. This work is unpaid and must be completed within six months of the sentence.

What do CPO perpetrators have to do?

- Participate in unpaid manual work in the community
- Be subject to periods of supervision
- Pay compensation to the victim, if necessary
- Be subject to specific conduct requirements to address reoffending
- Take part in alcohol, drug or mental health treatment, if required

Home Detention Curfews

Home Detention Curfews (HDCs) are enforced by electronic monitoring (tagging) and were originally used only for low-risk perpetrators serving less than four years. They are now used on longer-term prisoners, which causes some public concern. HDCs allow prisoners to serve up to a quarter of their sentence – for a maximum of six months – on licence in the community. Prisoners who fail to comply with the curfew or other licence conditions can be recalled to custody. The aim is to help the perpetrators reintegrate into society once they have served their sentence. HDCs help to reduce the prison population and are cost-effective. Sending a person to jail for a year costs about £34,000, whereas tagging a prisoner costs less than £2000.

The Scottish Government intends to expand the use of HDCs by using them for perpetrators on remand (perpetrators waiting in prison for their trial). Sobriety tagging will be used for those who have offended under the influence of alcohol. The bracelet sets off an alarm if alcohol is detected. There is little point in sending someone to prison for a few months for drink addiction if no action is taken to end this dependency. Individuals would also receive social work support.

The HDC service is run by the private company G4S in Scotland. The contract in Scotland is worth £13 million over five years. In England, SERCO has the contract and has faced bad publicity for issues such as charges for tagging that never took place.

Fines

Scottish courts have been encouraged to use fines as an alternative to prison sentences. This approach has been criticised for allowing prisoners to evade prison for offences such as assault. Moreover, a significant minority do not pay the fine, although in recent years new powers to crack down on fine dodgers have improved payment rates (see below).

FINE DODGERS BROUGHT DOWN TO EARTH AT AIRPORTS

Fine dodgers have been warned to pay up before they try to fly after a number of non-payers were arrested at airports in Scotland and England.

A man coming back from holiday in the Netherlands with a group of friends was arrested at Liverpool Airport over unpaid fines amounting to £770. The man, from Annan, who was returning from Amsterdam, had been fined at Dumfries Sheriff Court for possession of drugs and road offences including careless driving and had avoided paying since 2016.

His fine was settled by a family member but not before another member of the group of friends was also identified as a non-payer with an outstanding total of £600 in fines. He had unpaid fines for speeding imposed at Selkirk Justice of the Peace (JP) Court and paid up online.

A new report released by the Scottish Courts and Tribunals Service (SCTS) reveals that the fines collection rate remains consistently strong. It shows that 86 per cent of the value of Sheriff Court fines imposed during the three-year period between 1 April 2014 and 31 March 2017 has either been paid or is on track to be paid. SCTS Chief Operations Officer David Fraser said: 'The fines enforcement teams continue to be highly effective in securing unpaid fines. Failure to pay, or to engage with our officers, will result in strong sanctions being taken including arrestment of wages, bank accounts, your car being clamped or inconvenience and embarrassment by being arrested when travelling abroad.'

Three Glasgow men who found their bank accounts had been frozen paid up more than £2100 between them for fines imposed at Glasgow Sheriff and JP Courts for offences including assault, drug possession, drink-driving and having no vehicle insurance.

Advantages	Disadvantages
They are far less costly to enforce than a short-term prison sentence. The average cost of electronic tagging is about £2000 and a CPO around £2400 – less than half the cost of a three-month prison sentence.	One out of every three CPOs are not completed.
They allow the prisoner to atone for their crime by improving their local community.	There is the problem of enforcement and monitoring of the perpetrator. Lack of transport and staff can lead to limited community work by perpetrators.
Perpetrators avoid the stigma of imprisonment and being infected by the criminal culture in prison such as drug abuse.	The perpetrator may fail to carry out or complete the order. It is time-consuming and costly to take the perpetrator back to court for ignoring the CPO.
They enable the perpetrator to remain with their family and possibly prevent the break-up of a family. Many children end up in care if one of their parents goes to jail.	CPOs and electronic tagging have a poor image with the public and media. They are regarded as a soft option that fails to punish the perpetrator and can leave victims feeling that justice has not been done.
The reoffending rate is lower for perpetrators who receive a non-custodial sentence compared to those who serve a short-term prison sentence.	Many perpetrators who receive fines fail to pay. This means time and resources must be wasted chasing them up to take the perpetrator back to court.

Table 6.2 Advantages and disadvantages of alternatives to prison

 Show your understanding

1 Which of the four purposes of prison do alternatives to prison focus on?
2 What are Community Payback Orders (CPOs)?
3 Outline the arguments for and against CPOs.
4 What are Home Detention Curfews (HDCs)?
5 Outline the arguments for and against HDCs.
6 Refer to the extract on fine dodgers and answer the following:
   (a) Why is the use of fines criticised?
   (b) What powers do the authorities have to take action against fine dodgers?
   (c) Give examples of two actions taken against fine dodgers.

Debate

7 'Prisons are completely ineffective and should be replaced with non-custodial sentences.'
   Use information from this chapter and undertake research using websites and online news articles before carrying out a class debate about this statement.

 Added value

'Prisons are failing women.'

Consider the arguments for and against this hypothesis. Are prisons also failing men?

Chapter 7

Nature of social inequality

Social inequality in terms of social class, gender and race is not unique to the UK or Scotland and is a growing global problem as highlighted in two recent Oxfam reports (see below). The banking crisis of 2007–08, followed by a world economic depression and cuts to UK public expenditure (austerity measures) since 2010 have combined to widen this social inequality. Wealth and income inequalities have increased since 2008. Cuts to welfare payments have a greater impact on females and ethnic minorities than on the general population.

What you will learn:

1 The nature and extent of inequality.
2 The considerable evidence of social inequality published in reports and research.

Evidence of social inequality

Voluntary groups work to highlight and reduce social inequality (see Voluntary/charity group responses pages 93–4). Groups such as Oxfam, the End Child Poverty Coalition and the Joseph Rowntree Foundation provide evidence of the extent of social inequality as outlined below.

OXFAM 2017 REPORT: BUILDING A MORE EQUAL SCOTLAND

- The richest 10 per cent of the Scottish population live in households with a net income of more than £912 per week. In contrast, the equivalent figure for the poorest 10 per cent is less than £240. The figure is above £2608 per week for the richest 1 per cent.
- There are now more people in poverty in the UK than there have been for almost 20 years and a million more now than in the year 2000. At the same time, the richest 1 per cent of the population own 20 times more wealth than the poorest 20 per cent – nearly 13 million people – put together.
- Currently, one in five people in Scotland live in poverty. At the same time, the richest 1 per cent own more wealth than the bottom 50 per cent put together.
- In 2015–16 there were 880,000 people in Scotland living in poverty, including 190,000 children and 170,000 pensioners. The remaining 520,000 are people of working age. After housing costs are accounted for, more than 1 million people in Scotland are living in relative poverty.

OXFAM 2018 REPORT: REWARD WORK, NOT WEALTH

- Across the globe in 2017, the richest 1 per cent received 82 per cent of the wealth created.
- World inequality gap widens as 42 people hold the same wealth as the 3.7 billion poorest.

END CHILD POVERTY COALITION 2018 REPORT

- More than half the children in some parts of the UK are growing up in poverty and these areas have experienced the largest increases in child poverty over the past few years – a 10 per cent increase since 2015.
- This is due to the impact of the UK Conservative Government's benefits freeze (see pages 83–4).
- In the UK, 3.7 million children live in poverty, with 27 per cent living in low-income families.
- In Scotland, 232,000 children live in poverty, with 23 per cent living in low-income families.
- Bethnal Green and Bow in London's East End have the highest level of child poverty of all of the 650 UK parliamentary constituencies – a staggering 54 per cent.
- In Scotland the constituency with the highest level of child poverty is Glasgow Central at 45 per cent.

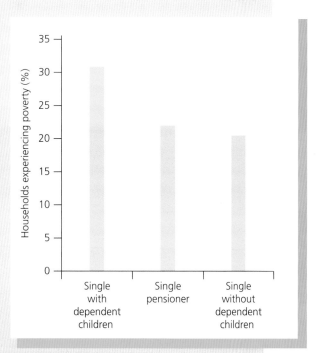

Figure 7.1 The top three types of UK household experiencing poverty

Relative poverty is defined as living in a household with an income 60 per cent below the median income. A couple with two children are living in relative poverty if they are living on less than £350 a week.

Absolute poverty is a measure of whether the income of the poorest households is keeping pace with inflation.

The **Gini coefficient** measures the degree of inequality in household income. In 2016 the UK figure stood at 34, an increase from 31 in 2014.

The Joseph Rowntree Foundation (JRF) is a charity and pressure group that provides support to those in need. The charity identifies the impact of government policies and provides evidence to challenge social inequality (see Chapter 11 for the work of voluntary groups).

JOSEPH ROWNTREE FOUNDATION: UK POVERTY 2017 REPORT

- Since 2014 an additional 300,000 pensioners and 400,000 children are now living in **relative poverty**.
- The rise in child poverty has been driven by stagnant wages for low-income families and a freeze on benefits and changes to tax credits (see pages 83–4).
- According to the Institute for Fiscal Studies, child poverty is estimated to rise to a record 5.2 million over the next five years, up from about 4 million today.

Case study: Inequality in Kensington and Chelsea

The Grenfell Tower fire in 2017 took the lives of 71 people and highlighted the vast inequalities in income and housing that existed in the borough responsible for Grenfell Tower. Below is some of the evidence of social inequality revealed by the local MP (Member of Parliament), Emma Dent Coad:

- Across the borough, life expectancy is the highest in the country but wide inequality exists. In wealthy Knightsbridge a person can expect to live to 94; in the area around Grenfell Tower this figure falls to 72 – a difference of 22 years.
- The child poverty level across the borough is 27 per cent, but in the poorest areas it stands at 58 per cent.
- Average income for residents of the World's End council estate in the south of the borough of Kensington and Chelsea is £15,000 a year, while home owners in a nearby upmarket estate have average annual earnings of £100,000.

Figure 7.2 The Grenfell Tower fire

Evidence of disability inequality

According to the UK charity Contact, in its report 'Caring More than Most', families with disabled children are more likely to experience deprivation as parents often have to give up work to become carers. This is made worse by the fact that one-third of disabled children live in a lone-parent household compared to 24 per cent of other children.

The three areas in Scotland with the highest rate of children with disabilities are Dundee, Glasgow and Inverclyde (almost 6 per cent of all families). Disabled children are twice as likely to live in families where no parent is in paid work (34 per cent compared to 17 per cent of non-disabled children). They are more likely to live in a household with no access to a car, in a home with no central heating and in overcrowded accommodation.

A report in February 2018 by the Demos think tank highlighted that more than a million benefits sanctions have been imposed on disabled people since 2010 – a far higher proportion than those for non-disabled people. Disabled people are far more likely to be sanctioned than non-disabled people, which suggests that they are being discriminated against.

Evidence of age inequality

- In 2016, over a million single UK pensioners depended totally on their State Pension and other income-related benefits for income. They had no savings or works pension. This is an increase of 26 per cent since 2011. Of this group, 3.2 million were women and 1.3 million were men.

- Pensioners are poorer than working-age people. However, they are treated better by the state (see page 85).

Evidence of gender inequality

- Men are nearly twice as likely as women to be employed in a top job – 10.6 per cent of men are in top management posts compared with 6.6 per cent of women.

- Women make up 23 per cent of board members of the top 100 UK companies.

- Only 23 per cent of professors at Scottish universities are women, despite women making up 47 per cent of the academic workforce.

- The gender pay gap has only slightly narrowed between 2008 and 2018.

- On average, for every pound a man earns, a woman receives only about 85 pence.

- Single mothers are almost twice as likely to be in low-skilled and low-paid work.

- Men have three times more in pensions savings than women.

Scotland's glass ceiling

A 2017 report by Engender, which campaigns for equality and women's rights, highlights that women are under-represented in the top posts in Scotland. The report shows that none of Scotland's top businesses (FTSE 100 companies) has a female CEO. Women are under-represented across a range of sectors.

In Scotland, women make up 52 per cent of the population but only:

- 35 per cent of Members of the Scottish Parliament (MSPs)
- 25 per cent of local councillors
- 16 per cent of council leaders
- 26 per cent of university principals
- 23 per cent of sheriffs
- 7 per cent of senior police officers.

Evidence of racial inequality

UK AUDIT REPORT ON RACE EQUALITY 2017

This report highlighted the following main findings:

- While state-educated white Britons in England had the lowest rates for going to university they were also less likely to be unemployed than ethnic minorities.
- Ethnic minorities were disproportionately likely to be on a low income, with almost half of ethnic minority households in the lowest 40 per cent (before housing costs were taken into account).
- Bangladeshi, Pakistani, black and mixed households were more likely to receive income-related benefits than those of other ethnic groups.
- Black Caribbean students are three times more likely to be suspended or expelled from schools than other students.

The **glass ceiling** is the invisible barrier that prevents women (and other disadvantaged groups) reaching the top in their chosen career. It is usually applied to barriers to senior management positions.

Show your understanding

1 Why has social inequality widened since 2008?
2 Refer to the two Oxfam reports, 'Building a More Equal Scotland' and 'Reward Work, not Wealth' on pages 47–8 and answer the following:
  (a) What evidence supports the view that there is a massive wealth gap in Scotland and the UK?
  (b) How many Scots are living in relative poverty and which groups are most affected?
  (c) In what way is social inequality a world problem?
3 Describe the terms 'relative poverty' and 'absolute poverty'.
4 Outline the evidence of social inequality in Kensington and Chelsea and of the people who lived in Grenfell Tower.
5 Describe the term 'glass ceiling' (definition) and the forms it can take.
6 Outline the evidence of social inequality facing the following groups:
  - disabled people
  - ethnic minorities
  - women
  - elderly people

Branch out

7 Using the reports from the End Child Poverty coalition and the Joseph Rowntree Foundation (JRF), and working in pairs, create either a poster or PowerPoint presentation highlighting the nature of the social inequality faced by many children and families.

Chapter 8

Causes of social inequality

Social exclusion

The causes of social and economic inequality are in many ways interconnected. The expression **social exclusion** links low wages, unemployment, poor educational attainment and discrimination (see Figure 8.1 on page 53). This term is used to explain the nature of poverty and its impact on individuals and groups. Not having enough money limits the lifestyle and opportunities open to the individual. Young people being brought up in a low-income family are more likely to struggle at school and have a higher chance of experiencing unemployment and poverty in later life. Those in social classes D and E experience greater poverty and reduced life chances (see Table 8.1). (The consequences of social inequality are covered in greater depth in Chapter 9.)

Being poor impacts on a family's involvement in their community. Their children may not be able to participate in activities such as school trips. This can affect their self-esteem and contribute towards a cycle of poverty. Individuals and families may experience a feeling of hopelessness and have low expectations of living a meaningful life. Ethnic minorities also experience social exclusion due to discrimination, racism and poor housing.

Social exclusion describes the impact of poverty on individuals and groups and the extent to which they are unable to participate in aspects of society such as education, health and housing due to being in poverty.

What you will learn:

1 The causes of social and economic inequality in terms of social class, gender, minority groups and age.

2 The ways in which employment/ unemployment, income and educational attainment all contribute to the cycle of social exclusion (social inequality).

Social class

A	Professional occupations
B	Managerial and technical occupations
C1	Non-manual skilled occupations
C2	Manual skilled occupations
D	Partly skilled occupations
E	Unskilled occupations

Table 8.1 Social class classifications

This is the traditional model that classifies people according to their social class. Vast inequalities exist between social class A and B, and social class D and E in terms of income and wealth, educational attainment and life chances.

Groups at risk of social exclusion

- Many elderly people are financially dependent on their State Pension and face fuel poverty (see page 57).

Many ethnic minorities experience discrimination, live in poor housing and have reduced employment opportunities. A significant number of the Grenfell Tower residents were from ethnic minority communities (see pages 62–3).

- Unemployed people and those in low-paid employment struggle with rising prices and cuts to welfare payments.

- Lone-parent families are at greater risk of poverty with the cost of feeding and clothing children on a reduced income.

- Children in the above groups may also be denied opportunities to go on school trips and family holidays and to access a home computer. They may also experience poor physical and mental health.

- Women are at a higher risk of being socially excluded than men. They are less likely to be in full time employment and more likely to be unpaid carers and to have a lower pension than men.

- Disabled people also experience isolation and discrimination.

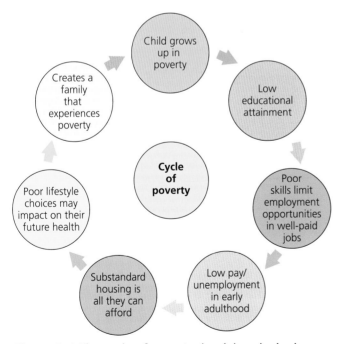

Figure 8.1 The cycle of poverty (social exclusion)

 Show your understanding

1 Copy out the definition of social exclusion.
2 In what way does social exclusion impact on families?
3 Refer to Table 8.1 on page 52 and choose the two groups most likely to experience social inequality.
4 What groups in society are most at risk of social exclusion?
5 Why is Figure 8.1 titled 'The cycle of poverty'?

Branch out

6 Working in pairs, create a poster contrasting the lifestyles of two imaginary families, one from social class A and one from social class E (see Table 8.1 on page 52). Refer to housing, type of employment and income, leisure activities, educational attainment and future prospects for children.

Unemployment, low pay and the benefits system

The Conservative Government believes that work is the best way out of poverty as it can end the generational cycle of unemployment. The Conservative reforms to the benefits system (see pages 83–4) are based on providing 'incentives' to the unemployed to move from welfare to work. Between 2013 and 2018 the unemployment rate in the UK fell from just under 8 per cent to 4.5 per cent, but poverty and social inequality did not decline.

Why has poverty not decreased?

- Most of the new jobs are low-paid, especially with the massive increase in employers using **zero-hours contracts**. The number of workers on these contracts increased from 168,000 in 2010 (when the Conservatives came to power) to over 900,000 by the end of 2016. If you are unemployed and refuse to accept a zero-hours contract, your benefit payments will be stopped. These contracts provide flexibility to students and retired workers but create job insecurity and very low salaries for workers looking for a permanent protected work contract.

- Low-paid jobs have led to a significant increase in the number of working poor, especially those with families.

- The banking and economic crisis in 2008 has led to a significant decrease in government spending on welfare (see Chapter 11).

- Many benefits have been frozen or have increased at a rate below the rate of inflation (see Chapter 11).

> **Zero-hours contracts** are employment contracts under which an employer does not have to state how many hours the employee will work per week and does not have to pay pension contributions or redundancy pay.

Gender inequality

Dramatic changes have occurred over the last 50 years in the economic and social position of women in society. However, despite these changes and equality legislation (see page 89), women have yet to achieve full equality.

Reasons for continued gender inequality

There is a range of reasons for this situation.

Work in the lower paid sectors

Women are over-represented in areas of the economy that are low-paid. Almost two-thirds of women are employed in twelve occupation groups. See Table 8.2 for more information about the representation of women in various job roles. Female-dominated occupations are often described as the five Cs: caring, cashiering, catering, cleaning and clerical occupations.

	Women (%)	Men (%)
Receptionists	95	5
Care assistants and home carers	88	12
Nurses	80	20
ICT managers	18	82
Software professionals	17	83

Table 8.2 UK occupational segregation, selected occupations

Traditional role as carers

Women tend to bear the main responsibility for childcare and domestic work. Many women switch to part-time employment when they have young children. If they have a professional occupation, they might lose out on or not apply for promotion. Women are also more likely than men to be carers for elderly or disabled relatives and then might only be able to work part-time at best.

Being a carer not only reduces an individual's income but also has an impact on their future State Pension and possibly their works pension. This explains why men tend to have higher pensions than women.

Lone parents

In the UK 30 per cent of families are lone-parent families and nine out of ten lone parents are lone mothers. Lone-parent families are vulnerable to poverty and many depend on welfare benefits, which have been reduced in real terms over recent years (see page 84).

The glass ceiling

This term describes the invisible barrier that prevents women (and other disadvantaged groups) reaching the top in their chosen career. It is usually applied to barriers to senior management positions.

The glass ceiling is created in a number of informal ways:

- Stereotyping and discrimination – some male directors have prejudices about a woman's commitment and ambitions, and may believe that having children is incompatible with senior roles.

- Presenteeism – this is the view that senior management must be seen working long hours. In universities, the glass ceiling can be blamed on a culture of long working hours, inflexible terms and conditions and pressure on researchers to produce academic papers, which can be incompatible with family responsibilities.

- Lack of role models – in some areas there is a shortage of female role models in senior posts to inspire women to move into senior levels.

Equal opportunity does not mean equal outcome

Many professional women who have small children prefer to maintain a balance between work and family life balance. This gives them the best of both worlds. By working, say, three days a week in a job-share, they have an opportunity to enjoy their babies becoming toddlers, and to be more involved as their children grow up, while still achieving work enrichment. So it is not always a question of male discrimination but of personal choice.

Race inequality

People classed as black and minority ethnic (BME) make up about 12 per cent of the UK population. The BME figure in Scotland is about 4 per cent, with about 44 per cent living in either Glasgow or Edinburgh. Glasgow's BME population more than doubled between the 2001 and 2011 censuses, from 31,510 to 68,684. The BME community across the UK consists of a variety of groups, including Pakistani, Bangladeshi, Chinese, African and other Asian groups.

While equality legislation and other government actions have improved race relations, race inequality still remains in terms of housing, income and employment.

Reasons for continued race inequality

There is a range of reasons for this situation.

Education barriers

A significant number of first-generation immigrants may face a language barrier. However, in recent years there has been a significant improvement in educational attainment among ethnic groups. In fact, Indian and Chinese students achieve better school grades than white students. Many BME graduates, however, work in non-graduate jobs, with a staggering 41 per cent of African graduates falling into this category. This might suggest that discrimination is a key factor.

Discrimination

Despite equality laws, many BME people feel that they are discriminated against in everyday life. Even high-profile Scottish politician, Anas Sarwar, a Labour MSP (Member of Scottish Parliament), has claimed that some fellow Labour members stated that he had no chance of winning the 2017 contest for leader of Scottish Labour because he was a 'black Muslim'. Humza Yousaf, cabinet secretary for justice, agrees with Mr Sarwar that 'Islamophobia' is a major problem in Scotland and the UK. Recent acts of terrorism in the UK have been exploited by some far right groups to stir up racial intolerance towards BME people. On BBC One's *Sunday Politics Scotland*, both politicians stated that racism and Islamophobia in Scotland were increasing. In 2018, a Labour councillor was suspended by the Labour Party for making a racist comment about Mr Yousaf. Anas Sarwar and Humza Yousaf have both received threats that their offices will be burnt down.

Figure 8.2 Scottish politicians Mr Yousaf and Mr Sarwar have experienced racial abuse

Low income and poor housing

Around 40 per cent of people from a BME background live in low-income households. As a result, many live in poor housing in areas of deprivation.

Lack of role models

BME people are under-represented in middle and senior managements posts in Scotland and there are very few BME police or judges, which can discourage these groups from considering these professions.

 Show your understanding

1 What, according to the Conservative Government, is the best way out of poverty?
2 Why, if more people are in work, has the number of individuals in poverty not declined?
3 Copy out the definition of zero-hours contracts.
4 Why have zero-hours contracts been criticised?
5 What are the five Cs of stereotypical women's work?
6 Why might a woman's traditional role as a carer be a cause of social inequality?
7 Outline the main causes of race inequality.

Branch out

8 Working in pairs, create a mind map outlining the main causes of gender inequality.

Added value

Research the debate that zero-hours contracts exploit workers.

Chapter 9

Consequences of social inequality

This chapter will look at the consequences of social inequality on specific types of individuals in society, on families and on communities. For a discussion around social exclusion, which can also be a consequence of social inequality, see page 52.

Consequences for elderly people

Austerity and budget cuts over recent years have adversely affected elderly people. In 2018, 16 per cent of pensioners were living below the poverty line – that's nearly 2 million people. Single pensioners are more likely to live in poverty than pensioner couples. The impact of social inequality on an elderly person can be

severe. Pensioners can become isolated, lonely and withdrawn from society, which affects their quality of life and health. Being in poverty also increases the chances of falling seriously ill.

> **What you will learn:**
>
> 1 The impact and consequences of social inequality on individuals (elderly people and children).
> 2 The impact and consequences of social inequality on families.
> 3 The impact and consequences of social inequality on communities.

Fuel poverty and elderly people

One of the problems facing many pensioners is fuel poverty. This issue has become increasingly well-publicised in recent years as energy prices have risen, leaving many households unable to afford to heat their homes to a comfortable level. Pensioners have felt the brunt of this, partly due to their incomes typically being lower than those of younger households but also because older people are likely to spend more time at home. Older people also require a slightly warmer room temperature in their homes. The official definition of fuel poverty is when a household must pay more than 10 per cent of its disposable income to heat their home to an adequate level. It is estimated that energy prices have increased by 37 per cent since 2010, which has led to dramatic increases in fuel poverty.

Figure 9.1 Pensioners are particularly affected by fuel poverty

The effects of fuel poverty can be devastating and can damage the quality of people's lives and health. The likelihood of ill health increases in cold homes, as illnesses such as flu, heart disease and strokes are all exacerbated by the cold. The need to spend a large part of their income on fuel means that fuel-poor households may have difficulty buying other essentials, which can lead to poor diet and/or withdrawal from the community (see Social exclusion, page 52). With many older people unaware of the potentially fatal consequences of living in poorly heated housing, every winter approximately 24,000 people die due to cold weather.

However, there are still many elderly people in the UK who are well off and have a very comfortable lifestyle. Many older people have paid into a private pension throughout their working life and have put money into savings and investments. Many older people also own their homes outright and so they have low housing costs – many bought the council house they were living in under the 'Right to Buy' policy in the 1980s. In some cases a pensioner may actually be 'asset rich and income poor', meaning that much of their wealth is tied up in their home. This often leads to older people downsizing from a family home to a more modest house or a flat, which then makes a cash sum available for retirement.

 Added value

Do the elderly suffer the effects of social inequality more than children?

Research this question and come to a conclusion.

Consequences for children

There were 3.5 million children living in poverty in the UK in 2018. Social inequality can have a devastating effect on children growing up. It affects their whole life, from their health and well-being to their educational attainment and aspirations.

Child poverty and educational attainment

Many students living in poverty go to school hungry, tired and in worn-out clothes. Many won't be able to afford school trips locally, never mind those to places further afield such as ski trips in the Alps or European battlefields. Not being able to afford such life experiences can narrow a child's world view and limit their educational prospects.

The attainment gap between children from richer and poorer backgrounds widens especially quickly during primary school. This is mainly as a result of differing parental aspirations and attitudes towards their child at school and material resources such as a computer and access to the internet at home. Reading charity Booktrust commissioned research into the reading habits of children and found that children from lower socio-economic backgrounds read much less. The study indicated that there are clear links between deprivation and not reading books, with parents from poorer households less likely to read with their children. It is estimated that five-year-olds from poorer families are about a year behind their peers in problem-solving and vocabulary.

It is well known that children growing up in poorer families tend to leave school with substantially lower levels of educational attainment (see also page 12). Such achievement gaps are a major factor in explaining patterns of social mobility and poverty.

In Scotland as a whole, just 42 per cent of students who came from the poorest 20 per cent of households achieved one or more Higher in 2016, compared to 81 per cent from the wealthiest 20 per cent. This clearly has an impact when a young person is thinking about a future career and the prospect of higher education.

 Show your understanding

1 How many pensioners live in poverty in the UK?
2 What are the various consequences of social inequality on elderly people?
3 What is fuel poverty?
4 Describe the effects of fuel poverty on elderly people.
5 'All elderly people are poor and in poverty.' *(Lucas Holt)*
   Give evidence to oppose this statement.
6 How many children live in poverty in the UK?
7 Describe three ways in which social inequality harms a child's education.

ICT task

Complete a project investigating social inequality in the city of Glasgow. When investigating life in the city, look at various factors such as population, poverty and lifestyle. Your project should include information on the following:

• the population/demographics of Glasgow
• levels of poverty in Glasgow – including child poverty
• the general health of Glasgow's citizens
• the lifestyle of Glasgow's citizens
• references page – at the end.

Use the Understanding Glasgow website for most of your research: www.understandingglasgow.com

Consequences for families

Over half of those living in poverty are from working families and most children in poverty live in 'working poor' families. Low-paid and part-time work means that families are falling below the poverty line even though there is a family member working. The Joseph Rowntree Foundation (JRF) suggests the gap between the minimum wage and the income needed to pay for a very basic household budget has widened. Low incomes and worklessness can bring considerable distress to a family. Families below the poverty line have to live on a tight financial budget and balance paying household bills, rent, debt repayment and food costs. Very little money is left over to spend on material goods or social outings. This in turn leads to social exclusion, with families struggling to participate in the goings-on of modern society.

Furthermore, the overwhelming majority (around 90 per cent) of single-parent families are women. Single-parent families are at twice the risk of living in relative poverty compared to those in dual-parent families. There is therefore a gender factor in the consequences of social inequality on families and, in particular, single-parent families.

 Added value

'Students who fail to achieve good qualifications when they leave school have only themselves to blame.' Prove or disprove this hypothesis.

Food poverty and food banks

Over the last decade there has been a growing need for people in poverty to turn to local food banks to provide emergency groceries and supplies. This indicates a growth in absolute poverty within the UK, with people unable to afford a basic necessity – food. In the UK families are going hungry, sometimes for days at a time. In 2017, The Trussell Trust reported that their network of over 420 food banks across the UK distributed 586,907 three-day emergency food supplies to people in crisis between April and September, compared to 519,342 during the same period in 2016. The Trussell Trust gave out 145,000 emergency food parcels in Scotland in 2017. Other food banks run by churches, community groups and charities are not counted in these figures (see also page 93).

Figure 9.2 Food banks provide food for people in crisis

People at food banks are more likely to have chronic health or mental health problems and to be socially isolated or withdrawn. Food banks provide more than just food aid as they can be the sources of a user's main or only social contact. The care and respect shown by food bank volunteers is often contrasted with the treatment people receive in agencies dealing with benefits and employment issues, where they can feel that they are negatively judged, not empathised with or understood, and not supported.

Reason for use of food banks	Percentage
Low income	28.49
Benefit delays	23.70
Benefit changes	17.73
Debt	8.53
Other	7.57
Homelessness	5.01
Sickness	2.86
No recourse to public funds	2.69
Domestic abuse	1.41
Delayed wages	0.81
Child holiday meals	0.76
Refused STBA (Short Term Benefit Advance)	0.40

Table 9.1 Main reasons for use of Trussell Trust food banks, 2017

Case study: The food bank was a lifesaver

Laura and her family hit a crisis when she was made redundant from her job, whilst at the same time her husband suffered a breakdown forcing him to leave work.

Their finances quickly plummeted and they lost their comfortable lifestyle just weeks before Laura was due to have a baby. They went from living in a suburban family home to a run-down concrete tower block.

Figure 9.3 Food banks are lifesavers for many struggling individuals and families (actors have been used in this photograph)

'Everything I knew and loved about our lives has gone. It's frightening. I can't sleep. I lie awake at night worrying that I'm not able to feed my family,' explains Laura.

Unfortunately, things then went from bad to worse. Laura and her husband couldn't afford enough food and found themselves skipping meals to feed their children. Between them they lost eight stone in weight and Laura was too malnourished to breastfeed her new baby.

Disastrously, a mistake by the benefits office then meant that sanctions were applied incorrectly and the family's weekly income was halved, something that lasted for three months. Laura said: 'I've worked for 25 years and there I was in tears at the Jobcentre with a baby on my lap being told we'd only have £50 per week to live on.'

The local housing association was so concerned that they referred Laura and her family to her local food bank for help. Laura says: 'The food bank was a lifesaver. I don't know where we would be without them. It meant we could eat together as a family for the first time in months.'

Laura is very grateful that the food bank was available, helping not just with food, but by offering a listening ear: 'The emotional support was almost as good as the food. It was just such a relief to finally speak to someone who cared and genuinely wanted to help. They gave us hope.'

Show your understanding

1 Explain the phrase 'working poor'.
2 Why could the impact of low pay and worklessness on families be described as 'distressing'?
3 What percentage of single parents are women?
4 Look at Food poverty and food banks on page 60.
   (a) How many people in Scotland relied on food banks in 2017?
   (b) Why are the figures from The Trussell Trust not an accurate representation of total food bank usage in the UK?
   (c) Beyond giving out food packages, in what other ways are food banks supporting people?
   (d) What are the three main reasons people are driven to use food banks?
5 Look at Case study: The food bank was a lifesaver, above. Describe in your own words how the food bank helped Laura and her family.

Branch out

6 Food banks are sometimes criticised for creating a 'dependency culture' where people take advantage of them. Do you agree or disagree with this view? Justify your answer.

Consequences for communities

Social inequality has long-term effects on communities. Socially deprived areas are usually materially deprived, run-down and lacking amenities, and have higher rates of drug and alcohol misuse and associated social issues.

Housing

Those suffering from social inequality often live in substandard housing. In the major cities around the UK there are high-rise flats that accommodate hundreds of poorer families. Within these tower blocks, flats are often affected by damp, which can lead to conditions such as asthma and respiratory problems in younger children. The following case study considers the Grenfell Tower fire of 2017. This case study is useful for understanding the consequences of social inequality on communities, families and ethnic minorities.

Case study: The Grenfell tragedy

At around 1 a.m. on 14 June 2017 a fire was reported at the 24-storey Grenfell Tower block in North Kensington, London. The fire, which started in a flat when a fridge-freezer caught fire, quickly spread as the outside fabrication of the building began to burn. A total of 71 people died in the blaze, which took more than 200 firefighters over 24 hours to extinguish.

Figure 9.4 Grenfell Tower fire

Grenfell and social inequality

Grenfell Tower was home to low-income residents, many of whom were ethnic minorities. Since its construction in the 1970s, Grenfell Tower has been considered 'social housing', which means that rents are maintained at a low level by law. It is owned by the local council, which is legally obligated to provide housing for people in its neighbourhood who are homeless or in need. The tower is located in a famously wealthy neighbourhood, Kensington, where house prices often exceed £1 million.

Before the fire, Grenfell residents repeatedly voiced concerns about fire safety in the tower, referring to the fact that there was only one escape route and no building-wide fire alarm or sprinkler system. They said their concerns were 'brushed away' by the Kensington and Chelsea Tenant Management Organisation, which manages thousands of properties for the council. Added to this, a multi-million pound 'upgrade' was made to the tower in 2016, mainly to improve its cosmetic appearance, given the affluent surroundings. The outside of the tower was fitted with low-cost flammable cladding, which is thought to have caused the fire to engulf the whole building.

The residents of Grenfell were poor and powerless – and they were the victims. Grenfell was situated just a few streets away from Notting Hill, an area with many expensive houses and apartments. Residents in Grenfell could not afford more expensive accommodation and were not wealthy enough to have an impact on the decisions that were made about fire safety.

→

The Grenfell tragedy was a grim and devastating consequence of social inequality.

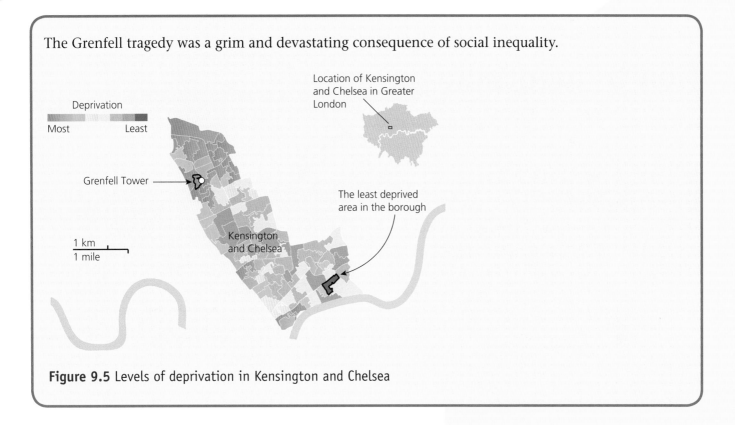

Figure 9.5 Levels of deprivation in Kensington and Chelsea

Crime

Another consequence of social inequality on communities is crime. The wealth gap in the UK between the rich and the poor has widened in recent years, with startling income inequality in 2018. Undeniably, those who are deemed 'poor' and suffer social inequality have their lives blighted by crime. Many argue that those from disadvantaged backgrounds have fewer educational qualifications and poorer living conditions, which can force them down a path of criminal activity. In areas where poverty rates are high, violent crime is prevalent. According to the Scottish Index of Multiple Deprivation (SIMD) the percentage of violent crime throughout Scotland is 2.5 per cent, in comparison to 5 per cent in the most deprived 15 per cent of data zones. Violent crime includes knife crime and crimes associated with gang culture, which are common problems in some of Scotland's poorer areas, such as Glasgow's East End. Antisocial behaviour in general is also more common in poor areas and is a consequence of inequality – a lack of amenities, money and role models combine to facilitate youths who engage in delinquency. In Scotland, those who are living in poverty are more likely to commit unlawful acts or be a victim than the general population as a whole.

 Show your understanding

1 In what ways can living in a tower block affect a child's health?
2 Look at Case study: The Grenfell tragedy.
   (a) Describe what happened on the night of the fire.
   (b) How could the tragedy have been avoided?
   (c) 'The Grenfell tragedy was a direct result of social inequality.'
       Give a reason to support this view.
3 Why do socially deprived areas suffer from higher crime rates?
4 What types of crime happen commonly in socially deprived areas?

Chapter 10

Health inequalities

What are health inequalities?

Health inequalities are the differences in the extent to which groups of people experience health problems and access health services, and how long they live. Research has shown that health inequalities are related to factors such as lifestyle choices, social and economic disadvantage, geography, environment, age, gender and race. Those who are most affected are more likely to have poorer physical and mental health than the general population.

People's life expectancy has almost doubled in the UK over the past 150 years, but there are marked

What you will learn:

1 The nature and evidence of health inequalities in Scotland and the UK.

2 The main causes of health inequalities.

3 The consequences of health inequalities for individuals, families and society.

Figure 10.1 Factors affecting inequalities in health

variations in the health of different groups. There are gaps between different socio-economic groups, geographic regions and ethnic groups, between men and women, between people of different age groups and between those affected by conditions such as mental health issues. For example, a girl born in London's Kensington and Chelsea area in 2016 might expect to live to about 90, ten years longer than a girl born in Glasgow in the same year.

While the overall health of people in the UK is improving, according to the Registrar General, over the last ten years health inequalities between social classes have increased because the health of wealthy people is improving faster than that of poorer people. Poorer people not only die younger, but also have more years of poor health and less access to good healthcare.

Evidence (see Fact files below) suggests that the causes of health inequalities include smoking, diet and exercise as well as poverty, housing, education and access to healthcare. These include both lifestyle choices, over which people have some control, and other environmental factors over which people have little influence.

Lifestyle choices

Are a person's personal lifestyle choices to blame for health inequalities?

Alcohol

According to NHS Scotland, alcohol sales data suggest that in 2017 consumption had increased by 15 per cent since 1994. In 2017, 17 per cent more alcohol was sold per adult in Scotland than in England and Wales. (The figure in 2012 was 19 per cent, so the gap is being reduced.)

The impact of this excessive consumption is estimated to cost Scots almost £4 billion each year for healthcare, which is equivalent to £900 for every adult in Scotland. Hospital admittances due to alcohol consumption have quadrupled since the early 1980s and deaths directly related to alcohol misuse have doubled. The impact of alcohol on crime and antisocial behaviour is equally bleak, with statistics showing that over 40 per cent of prisoners (including over 60 per cent of young offenders) were drunk at the time they committed their offence.

FACT FILE

Alcohol consumption

- Excessive consumption of alcohol contributes to health problems including high blood pressure, chronic liver disease and cirrhosis, as well as social problems such as antisocial behaviour and violent crime.

- Women in the highest household income group were twice as likely as those living in the lowest-income households to be harmful/hazardous drinkers (27 per cent compared with 14 per cent).

- Harmful/hazardous drinkers in low-income households consumed more units of alcohol per week than those in higher-income households.

- Scotland has the highest alcohol consumption in the UK and also the highest alcohol-related death rate in the UK. In 2016 the alcohol-related death rate for men in Scotland was 29 per 100,000 population, while England had the lowest at 17.5 per 100,000.

- Around 5 per cent of deaths in Scotland are attributed to alcohol.

Smoking

FACT FILE

Smoking

- There is a strong link between smoking and a person's social class and levels of deprivation.
- The 2017 Scottish Households Survey highlights the decline in smoking. In 2003, 28 per cent of adults smoked; the figure has now fallen to 21 per cent. However, the survey reveals that 35 per cent of people living in the most deprived areas smoke cigarettes, compared to only about 10 per cent in the least deprived areas.
- The 2017 State of Child Health report by the Royal College of Paediatrics and Child Health shows that 19 per cent of expectant mothers in Scotland smoked, compared to only 5 per cent in Sweden. In Scotland in 2015, over a quarter (25.9%) of women in the most deprived areas smoked following the birth of their baby, compared with 3.3% in the wealthiest areas.
- Around a quarter of all deaths in Scotland each year (13,500) are attributable to smoking.
- Smoking is responsible for around 33,500 hospital admissions every year.
- It costs the NHS in Scotland over £400 million to treat smoking-related illness every year.

Figure 10.2 There is a strong link between smoking and social class

Drugs

FACT FILE

Drug use

- The number of overdose deaths in Scotland soared by 23 per cent to 867 in 2016, with use of opiates such as heroin a factor in about 90 per cent of deaths.

- The number of drug-related deaths per year has more than doubled since 1995 – from under 400 to 867 in 2016.

- The highest number of drug-related deaths is in the age group 35–44 (38 per cent).

- The percentage increase in the number of drug-related deaths between 2002–06 and 2012–16 was far greater for women than for men (see Figure 10.4).

- In 2018 Scotland's drug-induced death rate was 50 per cent higher than the next highest European Union country.

- In 2018 Scotland's drug-induced death rate was 27 times as high as Portugal where many drugs have been legalised.

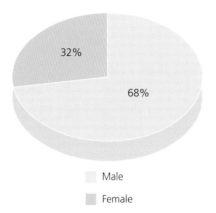

Figure 10.3 Drug-related deaths in Scotland by gender, 2016

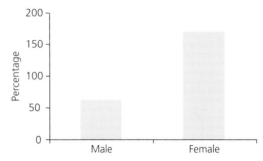

Figure 10.4 Percentage increase in drug-related deaths in Scotland by gender between 2002–06 and 2012–16

MORE THAN 700 BABIES IN SCOTLAND BORN ADDICTED TO HARD DRUGS

Recent research by NHS Scotland revealed that 729 babies were born addicted to the same harmful drugs as their mothers between 2012 and 2016.

These babies experience the same painful drug withdrawal effects as an adult. If the mother has been injecting, then the baby runs the risk of contracting HIV or hepatitis C. These babies also tend to be born pre-term and with growth restrictions.

Children who are born with this addiction have a higher chance of drug misuse as adults.

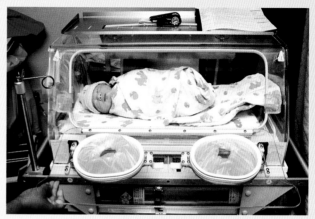

Figure 10.5 Babies born to hard drug users enter the world addicted to drugs and have to go through painful withdrawal symptoms

Obesity

FACT FILE

Obesity

- 65 per cent of Scottish adults were overweight in 2016, including 29 per cent who were obese. The levels of obesity in Scotland are the worst in the UK and among the worst in Europe.

- The amount of fruit and vegetables consumed each day by Scottish adults fell to its lowest level in 2016. Only 20 per cent of adults surveyed ate the recommended five portions a day.

- Children in Britain are consuming three times the recommended amount of sugar, with sugar-laden soft drinks being a major problem.

- Obesity levels in 2018 were more than three times what they were in 1980, when only 6 per cent of men and 8 per cent of women were obese.

- Obesity costs NHS Scotland about £600 million a year, with obesity linked to thirteen types of cancer.

- Over the last three years more than a quarter of all weight programme referrals for under-18s in NHS Greater Glasgow and Clyde – 103 out of 368 – were for children aged between two and four.

- Obese children are around five times more likely to become obese adults.

- A 2017 Health Scotland Report found that 22 per cent of Scottish children who began primary school in 2016 were overweight or obese. The good news was that this figure had remained broadly similar over the previous decade

- The 2017 Health Scotland Report also found that 6.6 per cent of children from the least deprived areas were at risk of obesity, compared to 12.7 per cent in the most deprived areas.

Figure 10.6 One in four adults in Britain is classed as obese

Show your understanding

1 What are health inequalities?
2 Which different groups are most affected by variation in health inequalities?
3 Why have health inequalities in the UK increased since 2008?
4 What health problems can excessive alcohol consumption cause, and what is the estimated annual cost to Scots of healthcare associated with excessive alcohol consumption?
5 Describe the link between smoking and a person's social class and levels of deprivation.
6 Outline the evidence to support the view that Scotland has a serious drug problem.

Branch out

7 Create a mind map displaying the main causes of health inequalities.

Develop your skills

8 'Deaths from drugs is a male issue as they experience by far the largest number of deaths and also have the highest percentage increase.' (*Harry Elliot*)
Using only Figures 10.3 and 10.4 on page 67, give one reason to support and one reason to oppose the view of Harry Elliot.

ICT task

Working in a group, focus on one of the following lifestyle issues:

- alcohol
- smoking
- drugs
- obesity

Prepare a PowerPoint presentation for the rest of the class outlining the impact your chosen issue can have on health.

Take notes during the presentations by the other groups on the other lifestyle issues.

Social and economic disadvantages: What is the health gap?

The Scottish Government's 2017 paper 'Long-term Monitoring of Health Inequalities' 'shows that Scotland's health gap is wider than anywhere else in Europe, and that the poorest Scots are expected to die 20 years before the richest, with men in the most deprived areas having a life expectancy of 68 which is only one year above the retirement age'.

Despite improvement in Scotland's overall life expectancy, the gap between rich and poor is widening and is wider than in the rest of the UK. There are still huge health inequalities in Glasgow. The head of the Public Health Observatory said: 'Life expectancy overall is getting better but the inequalities in life expectancy remain very stark.'

People in the most deprived parts of Scotland are four times more likely to die of heart disease before the age of 74 than those in the least deprived parts, and twice as likely to die of cancer. Among men, the 10 per cent living in the least deprived areas can expect to live until the age of 82, 14 years more than those in the most deprived areas. Women in the poorest areas live on average just 67.4 years, compared to 84.6 for those in the wealthiest areas.

On average, girls can expect to live around five years longer than boys in Scotland, although the gap is reducing. Male and female life expectancy is highest in East Dunbartonshire, which includes areas like Bearsden and Milngavie, and lowest in the Glasgow City Council area, which includes areas like Calton and Drumchapel. Males in East Dunbartonshire can expect to live for 80 years, eight years longer than in Glasgow City (72 years). Females in East Dunbartonshire can expect to live for 83 years, five years longer than in Glasgow City (78 years).

The gap in healthy life expectancy is even wider. Whereas life expectancy is an estimate of how many years a person might be expected to live, healthy life expectancy is an estimate of how many years they might live in good health. The gap in healthy life expectancy between men in the most deprived areas and those in the least deprived areas is about 20 years.

Scotland's poorest men will only be in good health until age 47.

Geography and environment

Does where you live cause health inequalities?

A 2008 World Health Organization report on social factors that determine health found that there were serious health inequalities in Glasgow. The report stated that a boy in the deprived area of Calton had an average life expectancy of 54 years compared with a boy from affluent Lenzie, 12 kilometres away, who could expect to live to 82. Sadly, these inequalities remain today.

In 2010, the journal *Public Health* reported on a study called 'It's not "just deprivation": why do equally deprived cities in the United Kingdom experience different health outcomes?' It went further and said that people from socially deprived areas like Calton had lower life expectancy and poorer health than people from similarly deprived parts of other cities in the UK, for example Liverpool and Manchester. They called this the 'Scotland Effect' or, more specifically, the 'Glasgow Effect'.

According to the Glasgow Centre for Population Health, what these reports show is that Glasgow is not alone in the UK in experiencing relatively high levels of poor health and deprivation. Liverpool and Manchester are two other cities that stand out in this regard, with high levels of poverty and the lowest life expectancy of all cities in England. In fact, all three cities share similar histories of deindustrialisation and have high mortality (death rates) associated with deprivation.

The conclusion is that shorter life expectancy in these three cities, and especially in Scotland, is not just due to higher rates of smoking and drinking and a poor diet, but also decades of bad political decisions. The reports claim that reduced life expectancy is linked to higher deprivation due to the decline of traditional industries, leading to high unemployment and depression. They attribute Scotland's higher mortality to the political direction taken by the governments of the day, and the consequent hopelessness and community disruption that was experienced as a result.

Other factors, such as alcohol, smoking, drug use, unemployment, housing and inequality are all important, they say, but income inequality, welfare policy and unemployment do not occur by accident, rather as a product of the politics pursued by the government of the day.

NATIONAL RECORDS OF SCOTLAND REPORT 2017

Life expectancy has steadily improved over the past three decades, increasing by 8.0 years for males and 5.9 years for females. The gap between male and female life expectancy has decreased. In 2017 a baby girl born in Scotland could expect to live for 81.2 years and a baby boy could expect to live until he was 77.1, a gap of 4.1 years. The gap in the 1980s was 6.2 years.

Other findings include:

- Life expectancy at birth in Scotland is 2.1 years lower than the UK figure for males (79.2) and 1.7 years lower than the UK figure for females (82.9).
- The number of males living to 100 years or older more than doubled from 50 in 2006 to 120 in 2016, while the number of females increased from 530 in 2006 to 790 in 2016.
- People living in more deprived areas of Scotland have a shorter life expectancy than those living in less deprived areas. For females there was a gap of 7.8 years between those living in the 20 per cent most deprived areas and those living in the 20 per cent most affluent areas. For males the gap was 10.5 years.

FACT FILE

Key points

- Health inequalities remain a significant challenge in Scotland.
- Social class impacts on health – the poorest in the country die earlier and have higher rates of disease, including mental illness.
- Tackling health inequalities requires action from national and local government and from other agencies including the NHS, schools, employers and third sector organisations (charities).
- Scotland's health is improving, but there are big differences between rich and poor.
- The gap in healthy life expectancy is wide.
- Men in the least deprived areas can expect to reach the age of 70 before experiencing any serious health problems, compared with just 47 years for those in the most deprived areas. For women, the gap is similar, 73 years for the wealthiest and 51 years for the poorest.
- Mortality rates from chronic liver disease in 2016 were nearly twice as high for men than women (19 per 100,000 compared to 11 per 100,000).

National differences

It has been emphasised that there are significant lifestyle differences between Scotland and the rest of the UK. According to Professor Alan Maryon-Davis of the UK Faculty of Public Health, there is 'markedly more smoking, bad diets and drinking in Scotland and Northern Ireland'. Compared with European Union (EU) countries, a Scottish boy can expect to live around four years less than a boy in Sweden and a Scottish girl can expect to live around five years less than a girl in France.

Health issues in elderly people

According to Age UK, depression is the most common mental health problem among elderly people. In 2016 it was estimated that there were around 2.6 million older people with depression severe enough to impair their quality of life. This number is expected to increase to more than 3 million by 2020. Loneliness is a major part of the problem. In December 2017 Age Concern Scotland stated that about 60,000 Scots would spend Christmas Day on their own. Brian Sloan of Age Concern said: 'The epidemic of loneliness among older people is having a devastating impact on their health and well-being'.

Dementia

According to Alzheimer Scotland, it was estimated that there were approximately 90,000 people in Scotland with dementia in 2017. Dementia is more common among older people, but can also affect younger people. Alzheimer Scotland estimated in 2017 that around 3200 people with dementia in Scotland were under the age of 65.

Race

In the UK today black and minority ethnic (BME) groups tend to have poorer health than white people. However, there are also health inequalities between these different groups, with some having much worse health than others. Evidence suggests that wealth and income differences among BME groups are the main factors causing race health inequalities, for example over 50 per cent of people in the Bangladeshi and Pakistani community live in the most deprived 20 per cent of areas in the UK.

The 2016 Health Survey for England showed that BME groups as a whole are more likely to report ill health, and that ill health among BME people starts at a younger age than in the white British population.

- Chinese groups have the best health of all ethnic groups in the UK, including white British people. Pakistani, Bangladeshi and black Caribbean groups have the poorest health, while Indian, Asian and black African groups have the same health as white British people.

- BME groups tend to have higher rates of cardiovascular disease than white British people, but lower rates of many cancers.

- In the mixed race group 25 per cent of men smoke, while only 16 per cent of Asian men and only 3 per cent of Asian women smoke.

Causes of ethnic health inequalities

Many BME groups experience higher rates of poverty than white British people in terms of income, benefits, unemployment, basic necessities and area deprivation. These factors can lead to health inequalities between and within BME groups. However, there are other factors causing health inequalities, such as the long-term impact of migration, racism and discrimination, access to healthcare and differences in culture and lifestyles.

Show your understanding

1 Describe in detail what is meant by the 'health gap'.
2 Does where you live cause health inequalities? (Use the evidence from pages 71–2 to support your decision.)
3 Outline the main findings of the National Records of Scotland Report 2017.
4 According to Age UK, what is the most common mental health problem among elderly people?
5 What are the major causes of health inequalities among BME groups?

Branch out

6 Working in pairs, create at least two bar graphs displaying information from the National Records of Scotland Report 2017 on page 72.

➔ Added value

'Lifestyle choices are to blame for poor health.'

Consider the arguments for and against this hypothesis. Does poverty play a part?

Responses to health inequalities

Government response

Health is a devolved issue and as such successive Scottish governments have used their powers to introduce a Scottish dimension to tackle health problems and inequalities. Between 2000 and 2010 the Labour Government doubled in real terms the amount of spending on the NHS. However, the austerity cuts imposed by the Conservatives between 2010 and 2018 to reduce public expenditure have placed severe pressure on the NHS. Budgets have been maintained but have only increased in real terms in the UK by 0.8 per cent a year in recent years.

> ### What you will learn:
>
> 1 The actions of the Scottish Government, private sector and voluntary sector to reduce health inequalities.
> 2 The effectiveness of these actions to reduce health inequalities.

FACT FILE

NHS Scotland

- NHS Scotland spent over £13 billion in 2018, which is 43 per cent of the overall Scottish budget.
- At some time in their life everyone in Scotland will make use of NHS services.
- Over 162,500 staff work for the NHS, including 60,000 nurses.
- Over 1.5 million procedures are performed in acute hospitals each year.
- Each year, 17 million GP consultations are held.

According to the Scottish Government 'There is a clear relationship between income inequality and health inequality.' In 2008 the Scottish Government's Equally Well Report introduced community planning partnerships between the NHS, local government and the third sector (voluntary groups) in order that they work together to tackle the link between poverty and poor health.

These are the main health initiatives introduced by the Scottish Government.

Measures to reduce smoking

The Scottish Government has taken decisive action to reduce smoking in Scotland. The most important action was the 2006 decision to ban smoking in public places. (England followed the Scottish example in 2007.) This covered pubs, restaurants and other public places. In 2017 it became illegal to smoke in a car if a child is present.

Figure 10.7 Smoking levels have decreased since the ban on smoking in public places

The latest figures from the Scottish Households Survey highlight the success of the smoking ban, with a significant fall in smoking. However, much is still to be done to reduce smoking figures in areas of deprivation (see page 66).

Free prescriptions

In April 2011, the SNP Government decreed that all prescriptions in Scotland should be free in order to help improve the health of the Scottish people. Prescriptions changed from being a **means-tested** to a **universal benefit**. Prescriptions are also free in Northern Ireland and Wales; people in England have to pay. Eye tests are also free in Scotland.

> **Means-tested benefits** are only paid out to those whose income and capital are below a certain limit. An example is Housing Benefit.
>
> **Universal benefits** are paid to all those who meet certain criteria, such as a certain age or disability. An example is the State Pension.

ICT task

Using the information in this chapter and your own research, list arguments for and against providing free prescriptions in Scotland.

Free NHS vitamins for expectant mothers

From March 2017 the Scottish Government has provided free doses of vitamins C and D and folic acid to all pregnant women regardless of income. Previously this had been part of the means-tested UK-wide Healthy Start Voucher scheme. The programme costs around £300,000 a year.

Minimum Unit Pricing of alcohol

Scotland introduced Minimum Unit Pricing (MUP) of alcohol in May 2018. The price was set at 50p per unit but is subject to consultation. This doubled the price of cheap drinks such as cider and high-strength alcoholic drinks. Prior to this, cheap alcohol was on sale at just 18p a unit. It has been estimated that a MUP of 50p will cut alcohol-related deaths by about 400 and hospital admissions by 8300 in the period 2019 to 2024.

For	Against
Prescription charges are a tax on ill health. If you have a long-term illness, such as high blood pressure, you will be paying for prescriptions until you are over 60.	Real cuts are being made in the NHS budget and funding can be increased by charging those who can afford to pay for prescriptions.
If you have to buy several different medicines, you might not be able to afford them all.	Free prescriptions encourage people to obtain medicine that they do not really need.
In the long run, free prescriptions save money as they improve people's health and therefore there is less pressure on the NHS.	Prescriptions for painkillers alone cost £31 million a year.
	In Scotland, 10 million prescriptions are issued every year, an increase of over 30 per cent since 2008.

Table 10.1 Arguments for and against free prescriptions

The battle to introduce MUP of alcohol

2012	The Scottish Parliament passes the Alcohol (Minimum Pricing) (Scotland) Bill to be implemented in 2013.
2013–18	The Scotch Whisky Association (SWA) goes to the courts to challenge the bill.
January 2018	The UK Supreme Court rules that MUP does not break EU law and as such can be enforced. The Scottish Government announces that MUP will be introduced in May 2018.

'For too long too many Scots have been drinking themselves into an early grave. It is no coincidence that as the affordability of alcohol has plummeted in recent years, alcohol-related deaths have soared.'

First Minister Nicola Sturgeon

Figure 10.8 Nicola Sturgeon

> We see this as a very positive step in reducing the deaths and misery created by alcohol. In 2016, 1265 individuals died from alcohol-related illnesses. Alcohol consumption in Scotland is far higher than that in England. Government intervention over cigarettes has led to fewer people smoking and this new policy will also save lives.

Doctor

Spokesperson for the drinks trade

> This new pricing will penalise all drinkers as it is estimated that 70 per cent of all alcoholic drinks will be affected by this new rate. The extra money raised will go into the pockets of the supermarkets and will simply increase their profits. It is an increase that will impact most on the poorest members of society as they have only a very limited income.

Sugar tax

In the March 2016 UK Budget, the chancellor announced a sugar levy on soft drinks to be implemented in 2018. There are two bands of levy: one for drinks with a sugar content above 5g per 100ml and a second, higher band for the most sugary drinks with more than 8g per 100ml. Drinks such as Irn-Bru®, Lucozade®, Pepsi® and Coca Cola® in their original form will have the tax imposed. A typical can of these drinks contains enough sugar to take someone over the recommended daily sugar intake. It is estimated that the new tax will raise £520 million a year, which will be spent on promoting healthy lifestyles.

The impact of this new tax has encouraged firms to reduce the sugar content of their drinks. To the consternation of some Irn-Bru drinkers, the manufacturer has brought out a new reduced-sugar product and scrapped the old.

Schools such as St Ninian's High, Kirkintilloch are setting an example by banning high-energy drinks from school premises.

Baby Box

From August 2017 all parents of new babies in Scotland are offered a free baby box worth £160. Based on a Finnish initiative, the box contains items such as clothes, blankets and toys and the box itself can be used as a baby crib. It is hoped that this will provide a secure start for struggling families and contribute to a reduction in infant mortality rates.

Other initiatives

- In 2016 the Scottish Government set up Food Standards Scotland (FSS).
- The Government's drug strategy Road to Recovery was updated in 2018 to respond to a surge in drug-related deaths. The strategy aims to ensure that drug users are in controlled treatment with access to methadone or other medication and to a drug consumption room.

Results of Government responses

The health of Scotland's population has improved:

- The death rate for heart disease and strokes has fallen by over 40 per cent since 2005.
- The cancer death rate is a third of what it was in 1998.
- Alcohol consumption has decreased since 1998.
- Since 2016 the annual rise in child obesity rates has decreased and the percentage of overweight and obese children has slightly declined.

Health inequalities do, however, remain:

- Coronary heart disease deaths among those aged 45–74 are over four times greater in the most deprived areas compared to the least deprived.
- Cancer deaths among those aged 45–74 are over 2.4 times greater in the most deprived areas compared to the least deprived. In 2006 it was 2.1 times higher – so health inequalities have widened.
- Hospital admissions due to alcohol-related illness are six times greater in the most deprived areas compared to the least deprived. The gap had been narrowing but it widened again in 2006 and in 2018 the gap was the widest it had been since 2003.

Why is overall health improving despite reductions in health inequalities not being achieved?

- Promotional campaigns on better diet, drink and lifestyle have had more impact on the better off.
- Improvements in preventive health measures have a far greater uptake among the better off. The uptake for preventive screening for bowel and breast cancer is far higher in the least deprived areas. This explains why men with, for example, prostate cancer, living in the most deprived communities in Scotland are nearly twice as likely to die from the illness as those in the more affluent areas.

- NHS Scotland blames welfare cuts (see pages 84–5) for its failure to reduce health inequalities. These cuts have a far greater impact on those suffering social exclusion. The impact of the reduction in welfare payments combined with the threat and imposition of welfare sanctions have had a negative impact on the health of the poor.

- A 2017 report by the Royal College of Paediatrics displays a clear link between increased poverty as a result of welfare reforms and the increase in poor child health.

Show your understanding

1 In what ways does the NHS meet the needs of Scottish people?
2 Describe the measures taken by the Scottish Government to reduce smoking.
3 Outline the arguments for and against free prescriptions in Scotland.
4 Outline the measure taken by the Scottish Government to reduce alcohol abuse in Scotland.
5 What other initiatives have been introduced to improve the health of the Scottish public?
6 What evidence is there to suggest that the overall health of the Scottish public is improving?
7 Why, despite the Scottish Government's best efforts, have health inequalities not been reduced?

Private sector and voluntary sector responses to health inequality

Private sector responses

The practice of patients 'going private' and paying for the services of consultants and private hospitals is longstanding in the UK. It is estimated that about 13 per cent of the UK public are covered by private health insurance.

This means that these individuals receive immediate treatment for their medical complaints, for example a hip operation to relieve severe hip pain. In contrast, NHS patients in Scotland who have severe hip pain have to join a long waiting list to see a consultant and eventually have an operation. From the first visit to a doctor and being referred for an X-ray or a scan to finally seeing a consultant can take as long as six months. Patients may have to wait another six months for an operation. In contrast, those who are covered by private health insurance or can afford the £13,000 operation are treated immediately. It could be argued that the present system is unfair.

In recent decades successive governments have formed partnerships with the private sector to provide a range of services within the NHS including:

- ancillary staff (cleaners and catering staff) employed by private companies
- the building and maintenance of hospitals by private firms via Private Finance Initiative (PFI) contracts (new PFI schemes have been banned in Scotland since the SNP came to power in 2007)
- NHS operations carried out in private hospitals.

These partnerships have been very controversial as the companies involved receive large amounts of money from the NHS. Critics argue that the NHS should not be run for profit. Supporters argue that carrying out NHS operations in private hospitals helps to reduce waiting lists. Scottish health boards paid private firms a record £82.5 million in 2016.

Case study: A tale of two health worlds

Ameena's story

Ameena is 65 years old and has severe pain in her hip. Below is the timescale for her treatment on the NHS:

Early August 2017	Ameena goes to see her doctor and is referred to hospital.
Late October 2017	She receives an X-ray appointment. Her X-ray highlights severe deterioration in her hip.
2 January 2018	Ameena's appointment to see a consultant is cancelled because the consultant is on sick leave. Meanwhile Ameena's hip pain intensifies and she is in constant pain and can only walk with difficulty.
Early March 2018	Ameena's new appointment is cancelled again. She phones to complain but no member of staff takes responsibility for the delay.
Late March 2018	Five months after her X-rays, Ameena meets with a consultant and joins the waiting list for a hip operation.
August 2018	Finally, a year after going to the doctor, Ameena gets her hip operation. What has taken twelve painful months can be done in twelve days for Mark.

Mark's story

Mark is 66 and works part-time as a solicitor. This gives him time to play golf. However, he is finding this difficult because of pain in his hip. He is still covered by his firm's private health policy. Below is the timescale for his private treatment:

Early August 2017	Mark has an immediate appointment with a consultant in a private hospital. X-rays are taken on the day and results confirm hip deterioration. Mark and the consultant look at their diaries and agree on a date for the operation.
15 August 2017	The operation takes place and Mark returns home to begin the process of recovery.
November 2017	Mark is now able to walk unaided and feels no pain in his hip.
January 2018	Mark flies out to Portugal to play golf with his friends.

The real cost of PFI hospitals

Many of Scotland's hospitals are under PFI contracts – over £260 million was spent in service charges in 2017, compared to £102 million in 2007.

The use of PFI schemes became widespread under New Labour to deliver not only new hospitals but schools and other public projects.

Figure 10.9 Edinburgh Royal Infirmary was built for £184 million under a PFI contract but will cost NHS Lothian £1.6 billion over the lifetime of the contract

Voluntary sector responses

Many voluntary groups work in partnership with local and central government to provide help to those with health needs. Groups such as Age Concern and Cancer UK also promote health interests by trying to influence the spending decisions of fund holders. This is a very difficult time for local community partnerships as the year-on-year cuts, especially to local council budgets, make it difficult to maintain council funding. Councils in Scotland have to make significant cuts to services and difficult decisions have to be made (see The end of the road for Meals on Wheels, page 81).

This limits the effectiveness of voluntary groups as some of their funding comes from local councils. While cutting financial support may deliver short-term savings, it will lead to increased numbers of hospital admissions and add further pressure on NHS budgets.

The Community and Voluntary Sector programme

The Community and Voluntary Sector programme aims to support, promote and influence the crucial health improvement role of the community and voluntary health sector by working with and through a number of key partners for delivery.

The programme has the following objectives:

- To strengthen and enhance the capacity of community and voluntary sector organisations (sometimes known as the 'third sector') to undertake work on health improvement and health inequalities

- To promote and support effective partnership working for health improvement between community and voluntary sector organisations and community planning partners – the NHS, local authorities and independent/private sector organisations

The following are two examples of area projects:

- NHS Fife project – working with community and voluntary organisations and groups to improve the uptake and reach of anticipatory care among people from 'harder to engage' segments of the community

- NHS Ayrshire and Arran project – developing referrals and improving access to the broader range of health and well-being services and resources provided by community and voluntary organisations and groups

Voluntary Health Scotland

Voluntary Health Scotland (VHS) is both a local and national network for voluntary health organisations in Scotland that encourages the public to volunteer their services to support those in poor health. The following are a few examples of the range of organisations within VHS:

- Alcohol Focus Scotland
- Arthritis Care
- Alzheimer Scotland
- British Heart Foundation
- Action on Dementia
- Cancer Research UK

Show your understanding

1. Look at Case study: A tale of two health worlds on page 79. Compare the treatment received by Ameena and Mark. Was this fair?
2. Outline the range of health services provided by the private sector.
3. Why have PFI hospitals been criticised?
4. Describe the ways in which the voluntary sector helps those with health needs.
5. What service does Meals on Wheels provide and why it is under threat?

ICT task

Working in pairs, choose a voluntary group that supports health needs. Create a PowerPoint presentation, with at least three slides, to outline the work of the organisation and the ways it helps those in need.

The end of the road for Meals on Wheels

The Meals on Wheels services that provide dinners to thousands of elderly and disabled people across Scotland is under threat amid concerns over its local government funding. The Royal Volunteer Service that provides these meals is reviewing its support as some local councils have not renewed their annual contract for 2018–19.

Age Scotland's chief executive stated: 'Meals on Wheels are a real lifeline for those who have difficulty shopping or cooking on their own, or are at a risk of malnutrition. Not only do they get a hot meal, but the social contact can be invaluable for those who are isolated and living alone. They can even help older people live independently in their own homes for longer'.

Chapter 11

Responses to social inequality

Scottish and UK Governments

Both the Scottish and UK Governments are committed to the principles of the Welfare State, which was set up in 1948. However, since 2010 the Conservative Government has reformed the social security system, partly as a response to the cuts made in public expenditure.

The Welfare State

In a civilised society such as that in the UK, the state has a responsibility to protect the health and well-being of its citizens through a national health service and a social security system. The National Health Service (NHS) is free at the point of delivery and our social security system looks after unemployed, disabled and elderly people. Our welfare state provides a service 'from the cradle to the grave'.

The Welfare State under Labour

The Labour Governments of 1997–2010 worked hard to reduce poverty and to improve living standards among those working and those unemployed. The National Minimum Wage was introduced for those in employment, and generous tax credits were provided for those in work. Jobseeker's Allowance was available to those unemployed, together with support from Jobcentre Plus aimed at assisting people into work by providing advice about job applications and job interviews. All families, regardless of income, received Child Benefit.

Labour also introduced the New Deal for Lone Parents to address inequality and to encourage more women with young children to return to the workforce. This was all part of Labour's New Deal to

What you will learn:

1 UK and Scottish Government responses to social inequality.
2 The effectiveness of UK and Scottish Government responses to social inequality.
3 The role of the private and voluntary sectors in tackling social inequality.

help different groups back into employment. The New Deal consisted of seven different unemployed groups such as the New Deal for Young People aged between 18 and 24, and the New Deal for Lone Parents. The New Deal ended in 2011.

Reasons for the Conservative welfare reforms, 2010–18

Economic

The banking crisis of 2008 led to a massive increase in government debt. The Government argued that the welfare budget was no longer affordable: overall spending on benefits was three times higher in real terms than it had been in the late 1970s. The decision was taken to make over £100 billion in public-sector savings by 2017.

Public support

Public-sector workers were forced to accept a three-year wage freeze followed by wage rises well below the rate of inflation. Other workers also faced restrictions on wage rises, which meant that public opinion polls generally supported the introduction of reforms to welfare benefit that would encourage the unemployed to find work. It seemed unfair that some unemployed families had a greater disposable income than those families in work. The Conservative watchword that the system should reward 'strivers not skivers' met with general approval.

Complicated system

The benefit system at the time was very complicated and not cost-effective. The plan in 2013 was therefore to simplify the system by amalgamating a range of welfare benefits into one single monthly payment called **Universal Credit**. It was argued that this would be cheaper to administer, reduce fraud and encourage those on benefits to find work and display greater financial responsibility.

Individual responsibility

Conservatives believe that the individual should take more responsibility for their actions. They argued that the social security system encouraged a dependency culture with some able-bodied individuals happy to sit back and receive state support rather than find work.

> **Universal Credit (UC)** was designed to simplify six means-tested working-age benefits including Jobseeker's Allowance, Housing Benefit and Child Tax Credit by combining them into one benefit. UC is paid monthly in arrears and includes Housing Benefit. Prior to this, rent was usually paid directly to the landlord. UC is being rolled out gradually across the UK.

Changes to the welfare system, 2010–15

In the period 2010–15, the following changes were made to the welfare system:

- **The payment of UC monthly in arrears** – this has made it very difficult for struggling families to manage their budgets, with many forced to take out payday loans at excessive rates

of interest. In areas of the country where UC has been introduced, food bank use has increased by 40 per cent, housing arrears by 15 per cent and requests for crisis grants by 87 per cent. In Stirling, rent arrears in the four months following the introduction of UC increased from £13,000 to £58,000 for UC claimants. This was partly a result of a six-week wait prior to receiving financial support.

- **The individual benefit cap** – the amount that workless households can receive in welfare payments has been capped. From April 2013, regardless of family size, the maximum a family could receive was £23,000 (£26,000 in London). The cap was lowered again in 2016 (see page 84). The Government regarded it as being unfair that a workless family could have a far higher income than a family in work.

- **The Claimant Commitment** – harsher penalties were introduced for those who fail to follow Jobcentre procedures. For example, the sanction for failing to turn up to an interview would be the loss of benefits for four weeks, which could have dire consequences.

- **The removal of the Spare Room Subsidy** – this was referred to as the 'bedroom tax'. Its aim was to encourage those whose homes were too large to downsize and enable a larger family to move in. Those in a house with one spare bedroom would have their Housing Benefit cut by 14 per cent and those with two or more spare rooms by 25 per cent. This, it is claimed, discriminated against disabled people who might have a spare room that was used by a relative who might stay to help. This new policy made it difficult for many vulnerable families to manage their reduced budget. This policy was abolished in Scotland in 2015, with the Scottish Government making up the shortfall in income.

- **Annual benefit increases capped** – benefit increases, except for increases in State Pensions, were capped at 1 per cent in line with annual awards to public-sector workers. Worse was to follow.

Figure 11.1 The cap on household income has had a serious effect on many workless families

- **Personal Independence Payments (PIP)** – previously known as the Disability Living Allowance (DLA), PIP is given to those living with long-term illnesses or disabilities. The Government claimed that PIP aimed to encourage disabled individuals to consider employment. All claimants of DLA have been reassessed to decide if they can return to work. Previously they would only have needed a doctor's certificate, but a private company is now paid millions of pounds to carry out these assessments (see page 92). Between 2014 and 2016 over 200,000 people with a serious illness or disability were declared fit for work.

The threat of being sanctioned and the lack of understanding shown by Jobcentre advisers has increased the stress levels of affected individuals, which can further damage their health (see page 78). As Polly Mackenzie, director of think tank Demos stated: 'Jobcentre advisers and capability assessors too often have a culture of disbelief about disability, especially mental illness.'

Scotland's cabinet secretary for communities, social security and equalities, Angela Constance, has stated that she feels PIP is 'deeply flawed' and is failing to treat people with dignity. Statistics from early 2017 show that two-thirds of claimants who challenge awards are successful.

A 2017 report by the National Audit Office found no evidence that sanctions were working. It also found a failure to measure whether money was being saved in this new system, especially when one adds in the millions of pounds being paid to private firms to administer aspects of the new system.

Welfare Reform and Work Act 2016

In 2015 the Conservatives gained an overall majority in the general election and announced further cuts in public expenditure. The UK Conservative Government's pledge to further reduce the working-age welfare bill by £12 billion by 2020 will hit the poorest hardest and widen social inequality. Below is a summary of the 2016 Act.

- The cap on the household incomes of workless families has been further reduced to £20,000 maximum, or £23,000 if you live in London. It is estimated that 90,000 families are affected by this Act.

Figure 11.2 Many disabled people feel that being reassessed is very stressful

- Working-age benefits have been frozen until 2020.
- Low-income couples starting a family after 6 April 2017 are no longer able to claim the family element in tax credits – worth up to £545 a year.
- Families who have a third child after April 2017 will not be able to claim Child Tax Credit for that and any further children. (This also applies to Child Allowance claims.)
- It is estimated that 13 million families have lost an average of £260 a year, with 3 million families losing an average of £1000 a year.

Other economic responses

In April 2016, the UK Conservative Government rebranded the National Minimum Wage (NMW) as the National Living Wage (NLW) for those over 25 and significantly increased it from £6.70 an hour to £7.20. A total of 1.8 million workers are now paid at a higher rate. Voluntary groups have been urging employers to introduce a living wage that is paid at a higher level, as paid by many local authorities. The campaign continues under the banner of the **Real Living Wage**.

Real Living Wage

While the UK Government's National Living Wage was set at £7.83 in April 2018, the Real Living Wage was set at a voluntary £8.45. This figure is based on the income needed to avoid living in poverty. Across the UK, 5.5 million workers (21 per cent of the workforce) are paid less than the Real Living Wage. The Scottish Government has urged the UK Government to pay this amount.

Age group	Amount per hour
NLW 25+	£7.83
NMW 21–24	£7.38
NMW 18–20	£5.90
NMW 16–17	£4.20

Table 11.1 National Living Wage (NLW) and National Minimum Wage (NMW) rates, April 2018

The Taylor Report

In February 2018, the UK Government stated that it would implement the findings of the Taylor Report into modern working practices and improve the employment rights of agency workers and those on zero-hours contracts. Under the recommendations of the Taylor Report, these workers will be entitled to holiday, sickness pay and the right to a payslip.

Elderly people

UK Government policies over the last 25 years have resulted in the number of pensioners living in absolute poverty falling from 50 per cent to about 15 per cent in 2018. Pensioners have not faced the same welfare cuts as other groups (see Table 11.2). Many own their own home and have paid off their mortgage. Also many have a private pension that gives them a healthy disposable income. The **triple lock pension** introduced in 2010 has ensured generous increases to State Pensions above the inflation figure. In contrast, many families have seen welfare benefits frozen (see page 84) and young people under the age of 25 have not been treated well. Those under the age of 25 are not paid the living wage, nor can they claim Housing Benefit.

Triple lock pensions: Pensions that rise along with prices, earnings or by 2.5 per cent, whichever is higher.

- There is now a significant income gap between poor pensioners whose only income is their State Pension (topped up by Pension Credits) and those better off pensioners who have a works pension.
- Until 2010 women received a State Pension at the age of 60. This gradually increased to the age of 65 for both men and women in 2018, rising again from 65 to 66 in 2019. The Government is planning further increases, which will raise the age of the State Pension to 67 between 2026 and 2028.

Universal benefits	Means-tested benefits
State Pension – the amount you receive depends on the contributions you made while in work or while you were in receipt of Child Benefit	Pension Credit – tops up a pension if you have a weekly income below £163 (for single people) or £248.80 (for couples)
Winter Fuel Payment – £200 for each household	Cold Weather Payment – paid to pensioners and households on low incomes
Attendance Allowance – extra money you can claim if you are over 65 and need regular help with your personal care	Savings Pension Credit – an extra payment to reward people who have prepared for their retirement by having some savings or income
Free television licence – for those over 75	
Free bus pass – for those above the female state pension age, whether male or female	

Table 11.2 Benefits received by pensioners

Powers of the Scottish Government

Welfare and income tax powers granted to the Scottish Government under the Scotland Act 2016 mean that for the first time Scotland can develop its own social security system (see Table 11.3). However, it will be responsible for only 15 per cent (£2.8 billion) of the present UK social security spending in Scotland.

Effectiveness of policies

Scottish Government policies to counteract the effect of 2010–18 UK welfare reforms have ensured that Scotland has the lowest level of poverty in the UK. According to the Joseph Rowntree Foundation (JRF), Scotland has the lowest levels of child and pensioner poverty in the UK. It also has the lowest proportion of people who are not in employment, education or training. Media coverage of the publication of this information by the JRF coincided with the resignation of the head of the Social Mobility Commission, Alan Milburn, and three other members of the Commission in protest at the UK Government's lack of progress towards building a 'fairer Britain'.

Welfare powers granted to the Scottish Government	Welfare powers retained by the UK Government
Winter Fuel Payments	State Pensions
Cold Weather Payments	Child Benefit
Personal Independence Payments (PIP)	The following benefits (now part of Universal Credit):
Carer's and Attendance Allowances	• Jobseeker's Allowance (JSA)
Severe Disability Allowance (SDA)	• Employment Support Allowance (ESA)
Industrial Injuries Disability Benefits (IIDB)	• Income Support (IS)
Funeral Expenses Payments	• Working Tax Credit
Best Start Grants (formerly Sure Start Maternity Grants)	• Child Tax Credit
Discretionary Housing Payments	• Housing Benefit

Table 11.3 Welfare powers in Scotland and the UK

The Scottish social security system will impose more flexible welfare rules. Those who fail to take part in preparation for work schemes will not be sanctioned and as such will not lose their welfare benefits. Also, claimants will be given the option of being paid twice monthly and of having Housing Benefit paid directly to their landlord. The Scottish Government has raised extra funds to reduce social inequality by raising direct taxation (its only tax-raising power).

The Scottish Government also hopes to use its welfare powers in the following ways:

- Extending Winter Fuel Payments to families with severely disabled children.
- Introducing a new Best Start Grant aimed at low-income families with children, offering financial support at key points in the early years (first child £600 at birth; subsequent children £300 at birth; two additional payments of £250 in the pre-school years).
- Introducing a new Job Grant in the form of a payment of £100, or £250 for people with children, plus a three-month bus pass for those aged 16–24 who have been claiming benefit for six months or more and are starting work.

Tax rates in Scotland

Scottish taxpayers earning more than £33,000 a year will pay more tax than all other citizens of the UK. An individual earning £50,000 will pay £824 a year more in tax than someone with the same income outside Scotland.

	Scotland	UK excluding Scotland
Starter rate	19% £11,851–£13,850	no band
Basic rate	20% £13,851–£24,000	20% £11,851–£46,350
Intermediate rate	21% £24,001–£43,430	no band
Higher rate	41% £43,431–£150,000	40% £46,351–£150,000
Additional/top rate	46% above £150,000	45% above £150,000

Table 11.4 Tax rates in Scotland and the UK, 2018–19

Show your understanding

1 What actions did Labour Governments between 1997 and 2010 take to reduce poverty?
2 You are a government spokesperson. Outline the reasons for the welfare reforms introduced after 2010.
3 What is Universal Credit?
4 Outline the impact of each of the following welfare reforms on individuals and families:
   - Universal Credit paid monthly
   - individual benefit cap
   - removal of the Spare Room Subsidy
   - Claimant Commitment
   - Personal Independence Payments (PIP)
5 What is the difference between the National Living Wage and the Real Living Wage?
6 Which group of workers do not receive the Living Wage and is this fair?
7 In what ways have pensioners been protected from welfare cuts?
8 Why are some pensioners far better off than others?
9 Copy out the following welfare benefits and for each state if the Scottish or UK Government is now responsible:
   - State Pension
   - Personal Independence Payment
   - Child Benefit
   - Winter Fuel Payment
   - Working Tax Credit
   - Cold Weather Payment
10 In what ways does the Scottish social security system differ from that in the UK?

11 Refer to Table 11.4 and answer the following:
   (a) Describe the new tax bands in Scotland.
   (b) Why have they been introduced and are they fair?

Branch out

12 Working in pairs, list the services provided by the welfare state for its citizens.
13 Working in pairs, create a poster summarising the Welfare Reform and Work Act 2016.

Scottish Government responses to educational inequality

Education is a devolved power of the Scottish Parliament. The SNP (Scottish National Party) Government has as a priority the reduction of the gap in attainment between schools in deprived areas and those in affluent areas. It also wishes to increase the number of students from deprived areas attending Scottish universities.

Educational Maintenance Allowance

All students from low-income families in Scotland who attend school or college receive a grant called the Educational Maintenance Allowance (EMA). (The EMA has been scrapped in England.) This encourages students to continue their education and, hopefully, improve their future employment opportunities.

Scottish Pupil Equity Fund

This is an ambitious programme to assist students and families in improving their attendance and educational progress. In both 2017 and 2018 the Scottish Government allocated £120 million to 2300 schools. The amount a school receives is based on levels of deprivation, calculated on free school meals entitlement.

The purpose of the Pupil Equity Fund is to raise attainment in schools with issues of deprivation. Schools have used the funds in a variety of ways, such as improving home/school links, high-quality targeted intervention, and literacy and numeracy skills.

University uptake

The SNP Government has set the ambitious target of 20 per cent of all those starting university in 2030 to be from the poorest 20 per cent of the community.

These are some of the actions being taken to reduce this poverty-related issue.

- Scottish students do not pay tuition fees; in England universities can charge fees of up to £9250 per year.

- Individual quotas to recruit more students from poorer backgrounds have been set for each university. Entry by students from poorer backgrounds to the new universities is much higher than to the ancient universities of Aberdeen, Edinburgh, Glasgow and St Andrews. Just 8 per cent of students from the 20 per cent most deprived areas attend these ancient universities, while 15 per cent of the students at new universities, such as Abertay, come from the most deprived areas. Further education colleges have a much higher intake of students from deprived areas, at about 23 per cent.

- Scottish universities have been encouraged to allow students with lower grades from the most deprived areas to be accepted. (These students will have achieved the new minimum entry requirements.) This positive discrimination policy has been hailed as a bold move to reduce social class entry inequalities. Others argue that it discriminates against middle class students who will be denied entry to a course despite having better qualifications.

Effectiveness of educational initiatives

It will be very difficult to ensure that children from deprived communities are able to achieve the same high-quality exam results as students from affluent areas whose parents are strong role models to encourage success and who can afford tutors to enhance their children's performance. In contrast, many children from poor backgrounds may face low aspirations from their parents and can be influenced by negative peer group pressure.

Success has been achieved in improving university interest and uptake from poorer students – since 2011 applications from students from the 40 per cent most deprived areas have risen from 28 per cent to 38.7 per cent.

Unfortunately the 2018 figures demonstrated a slight decline in university entry from poorer students, from 10.8 per cent to 10.4 per cent between 2016 and 2017.

Tackling equality issues
The Equality Act 2010

The Equality Act 2010 brought together the previous nine pieces of equality legislation, including gender, race and disability. The Act gives women (and men) a right to equal pay for equal work, even if different roles are being carried out. This is intended to break down restrictions in pay based on certain roles dominated by gender.

Women working for local councils involved in domestic duties such as catering have won court

---

Equal pay for equal work in the private sector?

Law firms have submitted claims against leading supermarkets using the Equality Act. The lawyers claim that (female) shop assistants are paid less than (male) warehouse workers, who can earn as much as £3 an hour more. If these claims are successful, the ruling will cost the supermarkets millions of pounds in backdated claims. There are different viewpoints as to whether the two types of work are equal:

> Our work should be valued the same as the men who work in the distribution warehouse. It is not fair that jobs carried out by women are underpaid. We are the face of our supermarket and we build friendly relations with our customers. We deal with customer queries and handle money. Also it is not just the warehouse workers who have to carry boxes. We deserve to be paid the same.

> We should not confuse equal outcome with equal opportunity. Women can apply to work in the warehouse and will not receive less pay than the men. So why do so few women want to work there, given that it means more pay? The answer is simple: we work in cold conditions with constant physical demands. If the same pay is given to both jobs, then I know which one I will choose – then there will be no one willing to work in the warehouse.

Lena, a shop assistant

James, a warehouse worker

cases against their employers on the grounds of discrimination. They argue that their work is of equal value to the work done by male workers, such as refuse collectors, who are paid more. Glasgow City had paid out just over £90 million by 2016. A second wave of claims had been submitted by 2018, which could cost another £500 million.

The Act also allows for positive discrimination. Job adverts can be aimed at different ethnic groups or at women. Employers can also identify these groups to provide appropriate staff development to improve their chances of getting a better job.

The Act states that from 2018 all companies with 250 or more workers must publish information about the differences in men's and women's pay. The BBC, as a public body, carried out an audit that identified a 9 per cent gender pay gap (the gender pay gap at ITV is 18 per cent). It also highlighted that the top-earning BBC stars are men and that female newsreaders and journalists were paid less than men. This led to Carrie Gracie's resignation as the BBC's China editor in January 2018. She subsequently received back payment and moved to work in a different BBC department.

Breaking the glass ceiling

In 2016, the Scottish Government set out ambitious plans that by 2020 there would be a 50:50 gender balance on public-sector boards. A significant number of women are now being appointed to these bodies; for example, in 2018 five of the nine directors on the board of Scottish Natural Heritage were women.

Universities Scotland has decided to remove the glass ceiling by having a minimum 40 per cent female representation on their boards of governors. Universities also support the promotion of women by taking part in Aurora, a women-only leadership development programme. There was a 39 per cent increase in the number of female professors at Scottish universities between 2012 and 2017.

The share of women directors in the UK nearly doubled in the decade to 2017, from 14 per cent to 27 per cent. Progress was also made in that the percentage of women in top posts improved from 5.9 per cent to 6.6 per cent over the same period. For those under 40 working full time there is a near zero gender pay gap.

Equality and Human Rights Commission

The role of the Equality and Human Rights Commission (EHRC) is to protect, enforce and promote equality in the nine key areas outlined in Table 11.5.

The EHRC publishes reports on the progress made in the UK in achieving equality. One such report highlighted the difficulties of disabled adults and BME women in finding work. All reports are sent to every public body and government department to enable them to develop strategies to avoid discriminatory practice.

In 2016, the Scottish Government and relevant voluntary groups set up the Race Equality Framework for Scotland 2016–2030. This will enable Scotland to tackle long-term systematic inequalities and respond to socio-economic challenges. An independent Race Equality Adviser has been appointed to coordinate future progress. In October 2017 the UK Government published a detailed report on a range of public services used by different racial groups to establish a strategy to effectively tackle race inequalities.

Age
Disability
Gender reassignment
Marriage and civil partnerships
Pregnancy and maternity
Race
Religion or belief
Sex
Sexual orientation

Table 11.5 EHRC's key protected areas

BMEs are outperforming their white British fellow students in achieving entry qualifications to universities (see Figure 11.3) and Black Africans are making excellent progress in ensuring that their children appreciate the value of a good education. In 2015, 68 per cent of black African students achieved five good grades in their GCSE exams, compared with 65 per cent of white students.

Other attempts to tackle inequality

The Living Wage (formerly the National Minimum Wage), Working Tax Credit and Child Tax Credit benefit women more than men. As a result, changes to these benefits have more impact on women. A 2017 House of Commons report indicates that a range of welfare cuts and new regulations impact disproportionately badly on women and BMEs. The total tax and benefit changes introduced between 2010 and 2020 are estimated to bring in savings of £94 billion. Of those, no less than £80.7 billion will fall on women – a staggering 86 per cent of the total. The Conservative Government has been accused of failing to undertake a gender audit of their own economic policies, despite requests from the House of Commons committee responsible for equality issues.

Effectiveness of UK Government responses

The UK has been very successful in reducing the number of workless adults and measures such as the Living Wage have improved the net income of the low-paid. However, these measures have not reduced poverty as the majority of new jobs are poorly paid, with many workers on zero-hours contracts. As a result, there has been a massive increase in the number of working families living in relative poverty. Eight years of cuts to welfare benefits have contributed to an increase in child poverty – up by 10 per cent since 2015. Child poverty in the UK is estimated to rise to a record 5.2 million by 2022, up from about 3.2 million in 2015 (see page 84).

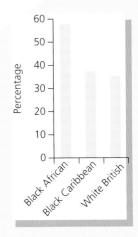

Figure 11.3 Students going to university by selected groups, England and Wales

Show your understanding

1. Outline the educational priority of the Scottish Government.
2. Describe the EMA and the Scottish Pupil Equity Fund.
3. Outline the targets set and actions taken to encourage more students from deprived areas to move into higher education.
4. To what extent have government educational initiatives been successful?
5. Describe, in detail, the role and impact of the Equality Act.
6. In your opinion, should women who work in the supermarkets receive the same wage as men who work in the warehouses? Give reasons to support your decision.
7. In what way does the EHRC promote and protect the rights of vulnerable groups in society, especially disabled people and BME people?
8. Give at least one reason why the UK Government has failed to reduce poverty.

Debate

9. 'Women who work in the supermarkets should receive the same pay as men who work in the warehouses.'
   Hold a class debate about this statement.

Private sector and voluntary sector responses to social inequality

Private sector responses

The private sector plays its part in responding to issues of inequality by providing employment and by taking part in Modern Apprenticeship schemes. All firms should, by law, pay employees aged 25 and over the National Living Wage. Those under 25 should receive the National Minimum Wage for their age group. However, some employers, especially in the catering trade, underpay their workers.

Some enlightened employers pay their workers the Real Living Wage, which is higher than the National Living Wage. Over 600 employers have signed up across Scotland and the UK to provide the Real Living Wage.

The use of private companies to administer welfare reforms is a very controversial area. Conservative governments have used private firms to assess the health needs of UK citizens as part of the Conservative ideology to encourage ill people to return to the workplace (and to reduce welfare payments). The Government claims that these Work Capability Assessments help ensure that people get the right level of support that they need. The assessments are being carried out to determine whether individuals are entitled to the Personal Independence Payment (PIP), which is gradually replacing the Disability Living Allowance (DLA). Since the process began in 2013 two private companies, ATOS and Capita, have earned more than £500 million carrying out these assessments (see also page 84).

Skills Development Scotland

Skills Development Scotland introduced Foundation Apprenticeships to help young people gain important real-world work experience and access work-based learning while they are still at school. This is important as unemployment rates in Scotland are higher for young people than for adults.

Skills Development Scotland offers a range of initiatives as outlined below.

Modern Apprenticeships

These assist employers to develop the skills of new staff and to update existing staff. Each year over 26,000 workers begin a Modern Apprenticeship, which combines a qualification with on-the-job training. There are over 80 different pathways, ranging from healthcare and financial services to construction and ICT. Modern Apprenticeships are available at four different levels, some of which are equivalent to a degree.

Graduate Apprenticeships

These provide work-based learning opportunities up to master's degree level for employees. The participant combines academic knowledge with appropriate skills development. The initial focus covers ICT/digital, civil engineering and engineering.

Voluntary/charity group responses

In Chapter 10 we looked at the valuable work done by voluntary/charity groups in meeting the health needs of individuals and groups. Figure 11.4 outlines the active work of these groups in supporting vulnerable people. They monitor the impact of different policies on social inequality and promote the needs of the most vulnerable in society. Voluntary groups work in partnership with local government and depend on the funding local government provides. However, all Scottish local councils have been cutting budgets and this is impacting on the ability of voluntary organisations to support vulnerable groups. In 2018, the North Ayrshire Advice Service announced its closure as a result of North Ayrshire Council's decision to withdraw funding. The service had helped vulnerable people in a range of ways, such

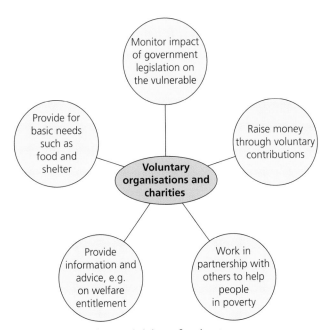

Figure 11.4 The activities of voluntary groups including charities

as completing application forms for benefits, writing letters to appeal against withdrawal of benefits and finding access to sources of income for those in dire need.

Some voluntary groups and their actions include:

- **Child Poverty Action Group** (CPAG) works to promote the interests of children and to monitor the impact of welfare reforms on their families. In autumn 2017, CPAG, in partnership with church groups, launched a campaign for an additional weekly £5 per child to be given to families that receive Child Benefit, with the aim of lifting many families out of poverty. The campaign, entitled 'Give me Five', was in response to the Government decision to freeze Child Benefit.

- **The Trussell Trust**, a Christian anti-poverty charity, gives emergency food and support to individuals and families who are among the 13 million people who live below the poverty line. In 2017, over 1 million people received three-day emergency food supplies at over 400 food banks across the UK. Over 90 per cent of food given out by its food banks is donated by the public. Between 2013 and 2018 there was a massive increase in the use of food banks.

- **Food banks** play a crucial role in providing not just food, but also comfort and support, as highlighted in a March 2018 report by Glasgow University. They have become an essential part of Scotland's welfare system with councils, doctors, housing workers and charities all taking them for granted. The report states 'People get something of their humanity back through the friendly treatment they received at food banks'. This contrasts with their experience of staff working in agencies dealing with benefits and employment issues, where people felt they were 'negatively judged, not empathised with or understood and not supported'.

Case study: Emily's story

Figure 11.5 Emily (an actor has been used in this photograph)

Emily's world was turned upside when her mother died. Her life became disorganised and she was sanctioned for missing an interview appointment. A mother of two, she quickly used up her savings and soon there was little food in the house.

Emily was nervous about going to a food bank, but it was the best decision she ever made. As well as providing food for Emily and her children, the food bank volunteers gave her comfort and the strength to get back on her feet, as well as valuable advice on benefit support. Emily's circumstances have now improved and she has signed up as a volunteer at the food bank. For the Emilys of this world, voluntary groups are essential and help to alleviate the impact of welfare cuts.

Show your understanding

1 What actions can employers take to improve the salaries of their employees?
2 Describe the range of courses provided by Skills Development Scotland.
3 What criticisms are made of private companies involved in social security decisions?
4 Describe the activities of voluntary groups in society.
5 Outline the important roles carried out by food banks.
6 Look at the Case study: Emily's story. In what ways did food banks help Emily?

ICT task

Working in pairs, choose a voluntary/charity group and create a PowerPoint presentation, with about five slides, to highlight the ways in which the group helps the vulnerable in society.

Chapter 12

National 4 & 5 Skills and Knowledge

Welcome to National 4 and National 5 Skills and Knowledge!

You should now have the skills and knowledge to complete the assessment demands of the Social Issues in the United Kingdom unit of the Modern Studies course. The skills and knowledge required for National 4 and National 5 level are very similar, with National 5 requiring you to handle more detailed sources and to provide greater detail in your knowledge answers.

Unit assessments and National 4

The summary on the next two pages is relevant to students who for whatever reason may not be proceeding to the exam itself, but who still wish to be entered and assessed for the standalone unit assessments, which no longer form part of the exam. For information on the examined assessment, please refer to page 103.

National 4 unit assessment

The National 4 award for Modern Studies is assessed by your teacher and not graded by an external marker. To achieve the award, you need to pass the internal assessment for each of the following units:

- Democracy in Scotland and the United Kingdom
- Social Issues in the United Kingdom
- International Issues
- National 4 Added Value Unit Assignment

National 5 unit assessment

While the National 5 course award is made up of externally marked assessments, some students may wish to cover the course over two years and may in S4 complete only the National 5 unit assessments. To achieve this award, you need to pass the internal assessment for each of the following units:

- Democracy in Scotland and the United Kingdom
- Social Issues in the United Kingdom
- International Issues

At National 4 you will be expected to answer a skills-based question/activity and knowledge and understanding questions/activities. For the internal assessment of this unit, the skills and knowledge that will be assessed are outlined in outcomes 1 and 2 below.

Outcome 1

- Ability to use a limited range of sources of information to make and justify decisions about social issues in Scotland and the United Kingdom, focusing on either social inequality or crime and the law.

Outcome 2

- Straightforward descriptions and brief explanations demonstrating knowledge and understanding about social issues in the United Kingdom, focusing on either social inequality or crime and the law.

Assessment evidence

Evidence for successful completion of both outcomes can be based on a range of activities:

- responses to questions
- a presentation
- information posters, or
- participation in group tasks.

For the Social Issues in the United Kingdom National 5 section, the skills and knowledge that will be assessed are outlined in outcomes 1 and 2 below.

Outcome 1

- Ability to use a range of sources of information to make and justify decisions about social issues in Scotland and the United Kingdom, focusing on either social inequality or crime and the law.

Outcome 2

- Detailed descriptions and explanations demonstrating knowledge and understanding about social issues in the United Kingdom, focusing on either social inequality or crime and the law.

Assessment evidence

Evidence for successful completion of both outcomes can be based on a range of activities:

- responses to questions
- a presentation
- information posters, or
- participation in group tasks.

National 4 Added Value Unit

The Assignment

The Added Value Unit will be internally marked by your teacher. The SQA's unit specification document states that in order to pass the Assignment you must research and use information relating to a Modern Studies topic or issue by:

- **Choosing, with support, an appropriate Modern Studies topic or issue**. You should choose an issue that interests you from any part of the course. Below are some examples from the social issues unit:

  - Free prescriptions should be introduced in England
  - Children's hearings are a soft option
  - The not proven verdict does not deliver justice
  - Poverty is the main cause of crime

- **Collecting relevant evidence** from at least two different sources. The section on research methods provides useful information on the types of sources that can be used.

- **Organising and using information** collected to address the topic or issue. You should use your skills to decide if the information is balanced or biased and based on fact rather than opinion.

- **Using the knowledge and understanding** you now have to describe and explain the key learning points you wish to make.

- **Applying your Modern Studies skills** in detecting bias or exaggeration, making decisions and drawing conclusions.

- **Presenting your findings and conclusion** on the issue you have chosen. You can present your findings in a variety of ways: as a written piece of research, or a poster, or a talk followed by questions, or you can use digital media such as a blog or journal.

See research methods section on pages 99–102 for more detailed information.

National 4 Added Value checklist

Name			
Title			
Section(s) chosen	Democracy in Scotland and the United Kingdom	Social Issues in the United Kingdom	International Issues
Relevant sources of information			
Number and type			
Evidence evaluated			
Skills used			
Detecting bias and exaggeration			
Making decisions			
Drawing conclusions			
Type of presentation			
Written report			
PowerPoint			
Wall display/Other			
Conclusion/findings			
Based on evidence			
Evidence of individual work (if task is a group/paired activity)			

Research methods

In Modern Studies we look at a range of issues that affect everyone's lives. These issues are based on evidence gathered through research carried out by a range of different people and organisations, from governments to charities. As part of your qualification you will be expected to carry out a piece of personal research on a particular topic that is relevant to what you have studied. This is called the **Added Value Unit Assignment** at National 4 and the **Assignment** at National 5.

How do I carry out a piece of research?

When researching a topic in Modern Studies, it is important to consider where you will get your information from. In the 21st century you have access to huge amounts of information, most of it at your fingertips on the internet. However, you need to be conscious of its accuracy and its likelihood of containing bias.

Where do I gather information from?

The information gathered from research can be broken down into two parts: primary information and secondary information.

Primary information

Primary information is evidence that you have gathered by yourself and is unique to your personal research. Your personal research should contain at least two pieces of information gathered by primary research, as well as information gathered from other sources. The ways in which you gather primary evidence can vary greatly, for example:

- surveys/questionnaires
- interviews
- emails
- letters
- focus groups
- field studies

Secondary information

Secondary information is evidence that you have gathered from research that was carried out by others. You should use it to help support your personal research. There are vast amounts of secondary information available in many different formats, for example:

- newspapers, magazines and books
- internet search engines and websites
- television and radio programmes
- mobile phone apps
- social media such as Twitter
- library books and articles

How do I plan my research?

In order to carry out a successful piece of personal research you need to plan it effectively. You will need to keep all evidence of your planning so that your work can be accurately marked.

Topic/issue

You should agree on a topic to research with your teacher. It must relate to one or more of the issues you have studied in your course, so it is a good idea to pick something from one of the three units you have studied:

- Democracy in Scotland and the United Kingdom
- Social Issues in the United Kingdom
- International Issues

Hypothesis

If you are being presented at National 5 and you have decided on your topic/issue, then you could state a hypothesis that you revisit in your conclusion. A hypothesis is simply a statement that your personal research will try to prove or disprove.

Sources of information

You may wish to consider the following questions about your primary and secondary sources:

- What useful information have I got from this source to help me research my issue?
- How did I collect this information or where did it come from?
- How reliable is the information gathered from the source?
- Could the source contain bias or exaggeration?

Background knowledge

What relevant knowledge do you have from your Modern Studies course that will help you to research your issue?

Conclusions

Using all of the information gathered, what are your final thoughts on your issue?

Presentation

How are you going to present your sources and findings?

You could choose from the following methods of presenting your Added Value Unit Assignment at National 4:

- **Oral presentation** – you may want to give a 5-minute talk to the class. This talk should be well-organised and can be supported with other materials such as a PowerPoint or Prezi presentation. You could include a question and answer session at the end of your presentation.

- **Written report** – you may wish to submit a structured essay/report or mock newspaper article. You could also create an online blog or wiki to present your findings.

- **Display** – you could create a large and well-structured poster incorporating your findings. After presenting it to the class you could hold a question and answer session.

- **Audio recording** – you could create a scripted podcast to present your findings. The podcast could include interviews or could take the form of a radio broadcast.

- **Video recording** – you may want to create a video recording to help present your findings. You could create a mock news broadcast or a short film, even using software such as iMovie or Movie Maker to aid your presentation.

Sample plan

Below is an example of how a piece of personal research could be planned and structured. You should work with your teacher to consider how you should plan, carry out and present your own piece of research.

Poster Presentation

Area of course: Social Issues in the United Kingdom

Topic/Issue: The effects of poverty on health

Hypothesis: *Poverty is the major cause of health inequalities in Scotland.*

Introduction: In this section I will explain why I chose the topic and how I collected my information.

Display: In my poster I will include four sources of information – the results of a survey/questionnaire, the transcript of an interview with a focus group, a section on secondary sources I used and, lastly, a section on my own knowledge.

This is what my survey may look like:

Source 1 – Survey/Questionnaire:

I am going to ask my friends, neighbours and family to respond to the questionnaire below. From the questionnaire I will create a bar graph of responses to the key question. I will then give some of the reasons for people's responses and discuss whether the findings of the questionnaire agree or disagree with my hypothesis. Using the questionnaire, I could also gather evidence to show whether people believe poverty is the major cause of health inequalities in Scotland.

Gender		Male		Female	
Age	12–17	18–24	25–40	41–60	60+
Do you think that poverty is the major cause of health inequalities in Scotland?		Yes	No	Undecided	
Give one reason for your answer					

This is what my graph may look like:

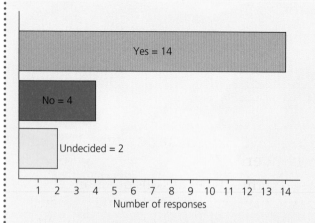

Source 2 – Interview with a focus group

Using my mobile phone, I will record a discussion session with a focus group of three of my classmates. I will ask the following question:

Why do people in East Dunbartonshire (where we live) live longer than people in Glasgow?

I will then type up a transcript of the discussion to display on my poster and I will highlight any arguments that agree or disagree with my hypothesis.

My transcript may look like this:

Me: Do you think that it is poverty or lifestyle choices that explain why people in East Dunbartonshire live longer than people in Glasgow?

(Life expectancy for a man in East Dunbartonshire is 80, and in Glasgow it is 72.)

Person 1: I think that poverty is the main reason as Glasgow has a greater number of unemployed people living on low incomes and in poor housing.

Person 2: I disagree, I think that lifestyle is more important – too many people in Glasgow have bad diets and do not exercise enough.

Person 3: But many people living on a low income cannot afford to buy healthy food or have a subscription to a health club.

Person 2: That's true, but I still think that people living on a low income could smoke and drink less.

Source 3 – Secondary sources:

In this section of my poster I will include a newspaper article on the topic that I have found and also evidence from the National Records of Scotland website. I will make sure to acknowledge the sources of these pieces of information.

Source 4 – My own knowledge:

The final source section of my poster will be based on my own knowledge of the topic. I will organise this into arguments that agree or disagree with my hypothesis.

Research methods: For each source I will consider its relevance and accuracy, and whether it could contain bias.

Conclusion: At the bottom of my poster I will present my conclusion, which will consider whether my hypothesis of *Poverty is the main cause of health inequalities in Scotland* has been proved or disproved.

National 5 course assessment

The course assessment is made up of two components:

- a question paper with activities from each of the three units
- the National 5 Assignment.

Course assessment structure

Component 1 – Question paper

The question paper is worth a total of 80 marks, with between 26 and 28 marks for each unit of the course. Overall, 30 marks are for skills and 50 marks are for knowledge and understanding.

Component 2 – Assignment

The Assignment is worth a total of 20 marks. Of these 14 marks are for skills and 6 marks are for knowledge and understanding.

Total marks available   100 marks

The marks you achieve in the question paper and Assignment are added together and an overall mark will indicate a pass or fail. From this, your course award will then be graded.

What types of questions will I need to answer?

There are three types of skills questions that you will have practised in class and answered as part of your course assessments. These are:

1 Using sources of information to support and oppose a view.

2 Using sources of information to make and justify a decision.

3 Using sources of information to draw and support conclusions.

In the knowledge section of your exam you will answer two types of questions:

1 Describe questions, for example:

   Describe, in detail, two ways in which social inequality can impact on families.

2 Explain questions, for example:

   Explain, in detail, why Scottish courts are now more willing to use alternatives to prisons when sentencing perpetrators. You should give a maximum of three advantages in your answer.

National 5 Assignment

The National 5 Assignment is a personal research activity that must include at least two methods of collecting information, with comment on the effectiveness of the methods used. The information collected should display knowledge and understanding of the topic or issue chosen.

The results of your research will be written up under controlled examination conditions. As previously mentioned, 20 marks are allocated to the Assignment.

Preparation for the Assignment

1 Research question

You should choose an appropriate topic or issue, for example, *The police in the UK should be armed* (see page 97 for examples of other topics). You may choose an issue from any of the three individual units or you may choose a topic that integrates two units of the course, for example, *The prison systems in both the USA and the UK are in crisis*. Best practice is to present a topic in the form of a question that has arguments for and against and that the public will have different viewpoints on. This allows one of the research methods to be a survey, and enables relevant conclusions to be made.

2 Research methods

As part of your Assignment, you must gather relevant evidence to support your hypothesis using at least two different methods of collecting information. There are a range of methods you could use, including surveys, reference books, websites, blogs or search engines. You are expected to evaluate the strengths and weaknesses of each research method you use and to analyse your findings. Remember that two methods are the minimum you are required to use, and you might wish to widen your range to more than two, *however*, you will only be marked on two methods in the assignment and your best two will be credited.

3 Research findings

This is the section that will display your detailed knowledge and understanding in describing and explaining issues relevant to your hypothesis, including the identification of a variety of viewpoints. Here you must **evaluate the evidence** you have gathered, **describe** what it shows, and **make a clear link back to your research** to gain full marks in this section.

4 Research conclusions

Once you have successfully analysed and explained the information you have gathered, you should make conclusions based on your research. Your conclusions must be relevant to your research issue and link back to your original hypothesis. Try to avoid simply repeating the findings you have previously given.